DAW 1/16 £13.99

How to Succeed at Assessment Centres

How to Succeed at Assessment Centres

By Kathleen Houston
and Eileen Cunningham

 macmillan education   palgrave

First published 2016 by PALGRAVE

Palgrave in the UK is an imprint of Macmillan Publishers Limited, registered in England, company number 785998, of 4 Crinan Street, London, N1 9XW.

Palgrave Macmillan in the US is a division of St Martin's Press LLC, 175 Fifth Avenue, New York, NY 10010.

Palgrave is a global imprint of the above companies and is represented throughout the world.

Palgrave® and Macmillan® are registered trademarks in the United States, the United Kingdom, Europe and other countries.

ISBN 978–1–137–46931–1 paperback

This book is printed on paper suitable for recycling and made from fully managed and sustained forest sources. Logging, pulping and manufacturing processes are expected to conform to the environmental regulations of the country of origin.

A catalogue record for this book is available from the British Library.

A catalog record for this book is available from the Library of Congress.

Printed in China

To John Houston, the legend – for allowing me to write without interruption. No one could have done more.

To Phil Cunningham for meticulously constructing and patiently explaining the numerical assessment examples. This chapter could not have happened without your knowledge, wisdom and generous giving of your time. Thanks, Dad.

Contents

Foreword

Contents

How to Succeed at Assessment Centres: The Essential Guide for Students and Graduates

Why you are reading this – celestial coincidence or a brilliant scheme?

If you're reading this, there's a good chance that you've managed something rather brilliant. You've hit the recruitment jackpot by being invited for an interview or assessment day. It may be that you are that wonderfully unusual and proactive person who has realised that you want to be successful in an assessment centre or interview process. As a graduate, there's a strong probability that this will happen to you.

Whatever your motivation, this book is intended to be your best friend and guide you through the often bemusing process that constitutes recruitment for graduate job roles. You may wonder why it has to be so complex and demanding. Well, graduate recruiters are really not out to make it difficult for applicants. They just want brilliant talent and they compete to snaffle the best. Think about how costly and miserable it is for an employer to make a mistake by selecting the wrong candidate. In the talent pool of great applicants, recruiters trawl with a big net. They have to be meticulous in sifting out the best applicants.

The plan behind this book is to talk you through what to expect from assessment centres and interviews in such a way that you will have experienced it in a 'virtual' way, normalising it, boosting your confidence and quelling fears. This guide/friend is like that cool person you know who has been through it all ahead of you and can make it all seem doable.

How this book will work

This book will offer a fast-track but measured approach to assessment centre and interview excellence. You will be in training for a brilliant career/life performance. The main focus will be to demystify the interview and assessment process, based on current research with employers and successful job candidates.

Students and graduates, try out the ideas and quick activities, following the chapter-by-chapter sequence, or dip into specific sections that tempt you. Whichever way you proceed, you will be more ready for the career marathon.

The employer perspective

Contents

Human beings have a habit of seeing things from a single, almost tunnel-like perspective. This is good when you need to concentrate on one thing alone. It has its drawbacks though. It can mean you take in just part of the information you need, without taking into account other perspectives. These other perspectives can be illuminating.

Perspective shift

Imagine this. You're lucky enough to have a beautiful house by the sea. You're happy to allow friends and family to use it but want to be selective about this. Think about this – what would be some sensible rules and expectations you might have about anyone who stays at your house?

Listed on the next page, in the left column, are some guesses of what you might expect as the house owner. Similarly, graduate recruiters have their own list of expectations of applicants – their vision of the ideal applicant. The parallels between your house and their company can be creatively mapped across as follows:

Job applicants compared to house guests	
House – ideal guest	**Employer – ideal applicant**
RESPECT Treat items/furniture/building respectfully.	'Like' the company. Know a good deal about it. Respect what it does.
ATTENTION TO DETAIL Leave it in a clean condition.	Your application shows you 'get' what the company is about, and you 'perform' in the selection process appropriately. You will represent it in a positive way.
INTERPERSONAL DYNAMIC Don't irritate the neighbours.	You show that you are 'likeable' and you connect well with other people.
GUARDIAN You will protect the house and make sure it is not burgled.	You will show your motivation for 'belonging' to that company/organisation and want to help it do well.

If you are thinking about applying for a job, it's a good idea to think about the company or organisation in this way. It will help you shift your mindset in the right direction. It will help you see things from the employer perspective.

What employers want

Graduate recruiters look for particular attributes (or personal qualities), skills and knowledge. Some attributes link to the 'respect' expectation, in other words, that people have shown respect for what they do. Other skills are reflected in the 'attention to detail' or 'interpersonal dynamic' expectations. You prove this in your application approach when you take the time to research an employer. This also suggests that you might be a good 'guardian' for the organisation.

The employer's viewpoint

It's easy to be very self-interested as an applicant for a job. It's normal to focus on the benefits of the job and what it offers. However, it's much more useful to view the process from the other side. Think about what you can offer an employer.

Getting into the mind of an employer will allow you to plan a more effective application strategy and campaign. When graduate employers are quizzed about what they want from applicants, their answers are less variable than you might think. In fact, employer 'wants' hold no real surprises.

There are some specific attributes, skills and knowledge, which are most in demand from graduate recruiters. These characteristics, often referred to as 'employability skills' are defined by the Confederation of British Industry (CBI) as follows:

> 66 A set of attributes, skills and knowledge that all labour market participants should possess to ensure they have the capability of being effective in the workplace – to the benefit of themselves, the employer and the wider economy.[1] 99

The key characteristics of the ideal graduate applicant, as defined by the CBI (2009), are shown in the following chart.

CBI 'Future Fit' employability characteristics	
Self-management – Having self-awareness and being in control of yourself	Teamwork
Business and customer awareness – Being commercially aware and understanding the customer or client point of view	Problem-solving – Identifying and exploring how to resolve difficulties
Communication and literacy – Getting your point across and taking other people's views on board – both in writing and in person	Application of numeracy
Application of IT	A positive attitude – Being proactive and confident

Rating yourself

Take a moment now to consider how you might measure up in real terms against the ideal graduate applicant. When have you demonstrated these particular characteristics or abilities? It's really valuable to track back in your mind through your life history (school/ sixth form/college/university, travel, interests, work of any kind). Notice when you might have displayed these characteristics. In the next exercise, you will have a chance to record your own examples from this time-travel timeline.

Self-assessment: Your unique characteristics

Think of examples of when you have demonstrated each of the characteristics listed below. These examples can be from inside or outside of education.

Self-management	Teamwork

Business and customer awareness	Problem-solving

Communication and literacy	Application of numeracy

Application of IT	A positive attitude

So how did you do with this? If you struggled to come up with examples, take a measured approach. Revisit your time-travel line. Consider school or college learning or other activities. Think about your part-time job or any volunteering you may have done. It's highly likely you used these characteristics at some point.

Here are some examples of numeracy, literacy or IT skills:

- You might remember working out ratios or percentages in maths or another subject such as geography or economics.
- You might have had to cash up at the end of the day in your Saturday retail job.
- If you were involved in Young Enterprise at school, you might have worked out your profits from a business project through a spreadsheet.

So what about self-management?

Can you remember a time when you had to control your temper or realised something about yourself?

Some examples:

- A teacher blamed you unfairly for something in class. You approached her later and calmly explained that it was not you who was to blame. (Self-management)
- You delivered a presentation for your A-level business course. The feedback from the audience helped you realise that you needed to speak up and project your voice more clearly. (Self-awareness)

What about teamwork and problem-solving?

It's not enough to say you were in a football team once. You need to think of how you played a part in a team success.

An example: Luke played in a hockey team that gained a place in a national final. He arranged the coaching sessions, selected the team and dealt with a team member, who dropped out with a last-minute injury. He had to solve a problem when the coach company maintained they had lost his booking for transport to the final in London. This situation required him to be motivational with others and make hard decisions. It also required him to maintain a positive attitude during the run-up to the final.

How could you prove you have a positive attitude?

Often this is demonstrated in a situation when something went wrong. Perhaps you failed your driving test the first time and had to bounce back and try again. Alternatively, you might have had to stay upbeat when something worrying was happening.

What about business and customer awareness?

University vacation work or part-time jobs offer a wealth of examples of these characteristics. Think about the commercial aspects of a job in a garden centre, for example. There are customer interactions, marketing opportunities for new products and the chance to develop an awareness of cash flow at different times of the year.

If you found you had some blanks in that first self-assessment grid, you may be able to go back now and add some examples. If you're still short of good examples, you can plan to seek out opportunities to develop the missing characteristics. Think about how you could do this quickly.

One way to develop valuable experience is through a patchwork of volunteering projects. Many charities will jump at the chance to offer you some skill-developing work. There are a multitude of short-term and one-off work projects you could undertake, such as these:

- Organising a fun run event. (business skills)
- Developing information leaflets. (communication and IT skills)
- Building drystone walls and fences for an environmental project. (teamwork)

Take a look at a website such as Do-It.org[2] for surprising ideas of great things you could do to benefit others and develop yourself. You can search for volunteer work locally through your postcode. You can commit a little time or offer an occasional stint with a range of organisations.

You might also think about some online volunteering. Did you realise that it was possible to gain volunteering experience with the United Nations without leaving home? Take a look at the UN Online Volunteering programme.[3] Think how good that might look on your CV.

This is all about recognising and developing the in-demand graduate skills. Next, get ready to showcase what you can offer to a graduate employer.

Your mission

Graduate recruiters often complain that applicants fail to demonstrate these characteristics. Your mission is to do the following:

- Prepare for the recruitment process.
- Strengthen and develop the required characteristics.
- Demonstrate them effectively so that you come across as the ideal applicant.

A good place to start in your preparation is to develop a real understanding of the graduate job market.

The graduate job market

The competition

In simple terms, it's worth realising this: you are not alone. This is not meant to suggest some disturbing vision of a mysterious universe with alien observers watching your every move. It's just that there are masses of applicants.

This is not meant to depress you. You are unique and special to people who know and love you. To those who don't know you, you are an unknown quantity. It's your job to make yourself known. So take a moment and guess the actual number competing with you for graduate vacancies.

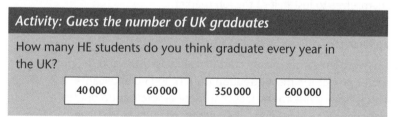

Activity: Guess the number of UK graduates

How many HE students do you think graduate every year in the UK?

| 40 000 | 60 000 | 350 000 | 600 000 |

And the answer is … 350 000 (*HESA 2014).[4] Clearly this number will fluctuate, but just for a moment, think of it in terms of the average attendance at a premier league match. This football crowd number is about 50 000, so the number of UK graduates every year is seven times the football match crowd.

Now think of yourself in the middle of all those fans, and you're all applying for graduate jobs. Got that? That's you and the horde of graduates.

How many graduate vacancies? Can you guess how many graduate vacancies there are to share amongst this crowd?

Working out the odds Graduate recruitment overall (the number of new graduate vacancies available to new graduates) has fluctuated over the last few years. However, it's worth doing a little bit of number crunching to get a sense of the job market for your skill set. You will need to get to know the broad make-up of the graduate job market. Think of it as four main sectors, a bit like the sections or aisles in a supermarket.

Graduate job supermarket	
There are four main sectors or types of employers.	
Large	Employ over 250 staff
Small/Medium	Employ 50–250 staff
Public sector	Government-funded agencies/ departments
Third sector	Charities and not-for-profit organisations

Unfortunately, many graduates are shopping for jobs in one or two sections of the supermarket only. They are therefore limiting themselves to just half of the job market.

Question: What's your guess about which sectors attract the most applicants?

Answer: The large, mostly commercial employers and the public sector attract the most attention from graduate applicants.
This is largely due to the fact that these employers go out to universities (careers fairs – often called 'the milk round') and actively talent-trawl for great applicants.

Another question: How many vacancies on average do large commercial and public sector employers account for in the graduate labour market?

Activity: Guess the number of vacancies

1. Take a look at the numbers in the boxes below.
2. Decide how many graduate vacancies are advertised through the larger organisations.

100 000	80 000	18 000	10 000

Answer: The most recent figures (2014,[5] based on the 2011–2012 graduate recruitment period) provide the following number:

18 300 possible vacancies.

Remember the number of graduates in the horde? It is roughly 350 000. So, if all of those compete for the 18 000-odd vacancies, the ratio of applicants to vacancies is roughly:

19 applicants for each vacancy.

Newspaper headlines often proclaim much larger applicant-to-graduate vacancy ratios (85 applicants for each job – Association of Graduate Recruiters [AGR 2013][6] estimate, or 160 applicants for each job [High Fliers Research 2013]).[7]

Analysis of the sources for these figures reveals the following:

- These numbers are generally based on applications for large organisations (those employing over 250 staff).
- The numbers quoted often relate to specific, often popular large employers.

So, there aren't actually 19 applicants or more for each vacancy, but:

19 applicants or more for each vacancy with large employers.

The forgotten sectors Remember those other sectors in the graduate jobs supermarket. In fact, 99.9% of private sector businesses in the UK are small and medium-sized enterprises or companies[8] (often referred to as SMEs). SMEs will receive fewer applications and yet are often a source of interesting graduate jobs. However, most graduates are chasing jobs in larger organisations. Typically, the odds are so much better if you target these other sectors *instead of, or as well as*, the large employers and public sector.

Beating the odds In order to get ahead of your competition, you will need to be successful at:

- locating the graduate jobs that you find interesting and
- making successful, convincing applications.

Follow the advice on the next page to boost your chances.

Chapter 1

Good applications: Three ways to beat the odds

Research the job market expansively, and make sure you are targeting the full range of employers (not just the larger companies/organisations).

Use resources such as the Sunday Times 100 Best Companies, the 100 Best Small Companies and the 100 Best Not-for-Profit Companies[9] and Glassdoor[10] to research the full range of employers you want to target.

Learn how to present yourself as the ideal applicant by seeing the process from the employer point of view.

Pay attention to what employers say they want, and show how you match this.

So, having started to understand the employer perspective and the graduate job market, it's time to consider the recruitment methods used by employers. You've probably heard about job interviews, but assessment centres may be less familiar to you.

Why interviews and assessment centres?

You might be wondering why it has taken so long to get to this point. It's really useful to understand the key elements of the graduate job market so that you can plan to be successful, even when the competition is tough.

As there's no shortage of applicants, employers need to use extremely rigorous recruitment processes. Whatever method they use to select staff, it has to be effective in identifying the best candidates. Assessment centres and interviews are a big part of this. Previously, an interview alone might have been used to choose the best applicant, but is this enough?

Why not just an interview?

Most people understand the idea of a job interview, even if they have little or bad experience of interviews. Recruiters use interviews as a short-cut process to get to know someone quickly. It might not seem like a getting-to-know-you process. For some, it seems like an intimidating interrogation.

However, employers have realised that interviewing as a means of choosing the best applicant is a hit-and-miss approach. Even when conducted in a methodical way, interviews can be imprecise in determining the best candidate for a job role. They may favour certain types of personality and even disadvantage really promising applicants.

As a result, recruiters have sought out different and additional ways to select the best applicants. Interviews are generally just a part of this process.

A moment in time

Interviews are very much a small window in time, allowing a glimpse of an applicant. A formal definition for an interview as part of a recruitment process might be:

> A structured dialogue between a recruiter and an applicant, made up of questions and answers, that ascertain an applicant's suitability for a specific job role, assessed against the criteria in the role profile.

This definition suggests something planned and purposeful, objective and fair. Good interviews will be aimed at this kind of process. However, interviews alone (to recruit someone) are actually very poor predictors of the most suitable applicants. In fact, occupational psychologists refer to this low success rate for interviews as 'low predictive validity'. This just means that there is no strongly valid reason for using an interview alone as a way of choosing the best applicant.

Beyond the interview

Assessment centres or assessment days are set up to help recruiters gain a fuller, more rounded picture of individual applicants. They are meant to give you the opportunity to shine by more than a one-off interview.

Although they are intended to be a fairer way of assessing a candidate, you can imagine that the stress is magnified because you have to 'perform' well throughout an extended time period. It can be exhausting.

Nonetheless, it is more than likely that you will find yourself assessed in some way for a graduate role, probably via an assessment centre and/or interview.

You are a revelation

Simply put, an assessment centre process is just a way for an employer to assess the suitability of a group of applicants in one longer session. It is planned in such a way that each part of this process (various activities, including an interview) reveals something significant about each candidate's motivation, skills and strengths.

This 'assessment' process is scored and recorded by assessors so candidates can be compared one against another. Each candidate is assigned a rating for each activity. Those with the highest overall ratings will be offered jobs. As a result, the 'best' applicant or applicants should be revealed.

Whatever you think about this, it is certainly worth finding out what to expect. There's good evidence that knowing what to expect is the best preparation.

The format assessment centres use

Most assessment centres use similar activities to assess applicants over a day or half day. The beginning might go something like this.

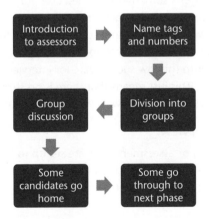

The selection process can be broadly the same and yet different for jobs in different sectors. For example, a legal firm might set up activities involving a legal terminology test, a presentation and a written report. A retail employer might ask applicants to assess a new product range, analyse some trend predictions and role-play a conversation with a supplier.

Here's how a large company recruiter describes this. Beth Jenkins, a Recruitment and Marketing Advisor, is speaking about the Shell International recruitment day (their assessment centre), but it is typical of many organisations.

Doing the research, Beth recommends, will really help you know what a company expects of applicants.

Employer's view – Beth Jenkins, Recruitment and Marketing Advisor, Shell International

The Shell recruitment day features a series of final assessed individual and group exercises. It includes an online exercise, a written exercise, a group discussion, a self-reflection interview and a presentation-based case study that includes a presentation and a final interview.

Throughout all these stages Shell assesses candidates based on *capacity, achievement and relationship-building skills.* These are detailed on www.shell.com/graduate, and it's really important to be clear on how you can demonstrate these at each stage.

Designing a selection process

Now try this. Imagine that you have to design a selection process. It's really useful to think about how you might approach selecting the right person for a job role. It helps you see things from a different perspective. In this next activity, you will have the chance to do this.

Self-assessment: Your assessment centre

Design the activities you would use at a TV company to choose a children's presenter.

1. Identify the skills and knowledge the person would need.

Skills	Knowledge

Self-assessment: Your assessment centre (continued)

2. List the best four activities you would use to test out these attributes.

Possible assessment exercises

- Panel interview
- 5-minute presentation
- 30-minute 'screen test'
- Numerical test
- Interview with children
- Timed research

- Group exercise/challenge
- Written test on current affairs
- Verbal ability test
- Prioritisation exercise
- Role play
- One-to-one interview

The four activities you would use:

_____

_____

_____

_____

Hopefully, you chose a mixture of activities which would test the specific skills and knowledge you identified. It is likely that these would involve

- a screen test;
- a research activity;
- written tests; and
- an interview with a panel.

As you can see from the exercise above, activities in good assessment centres are not chosen at random. They are based on the job criteria, skills and knowledge most required for that role.

Getting it wrong as a recruiter

Essentially, recruiters are pretty afraid of landing themselves with a 'bad' employee because it wastes time and can affect the performance of teams and individuals in that organisation *and* sabotage its success.

Getting it right as an applicant

Whatever activity you undertake, aim to demonstrate the attributes required. At the same time, stay true to yourself in any way you can. It is a careful balancing act.

My Advice – Maya Dibley,

Associate Publisher, Hearst Magazines, UK

Allow your personality and passions to shine out. It may end up being the opposite of what an employer is looking for, but if you act falsely and get the job, you'll soon find you aren't the right fit in the team.

Summary of key points

Understand what graduate employers want: Graduate employers expect you to present yourself in a way that shows that you have done your research and know their reputation and purpose.

Know the job market: The graduate job market has many interesting job roles to offer with large small, public and third-sector employers. Be sure to check them all out.

Be prepared: You can make sure you stand out from the competition by being thoroughly prepared.

Be ready to be assessed: Assessment centres and interviews are standard ways to recruit talented graduates. They can be a little intimidating, but you can train yourself to perform well by knowing what to expect.

Find out more

The following websites contain information on what assessments are and why they're used by employers:

- **Brunel University**
  www.brunel.ac.uk
  Assessment Centres – why and how employers use assessment centres

http://www.brunel.ac.uk/pcc/secure/Destinations/units/unit-ac005
.shtml

● **Psychometric Success**
www.psychometric-success.com
Who Uses the Assessment Centre?
http://www.psychometric-success.com/assessment-centers/
acfaq-who-uses.htm

● **Prospects**
www.prospects.ac.uk
Interview tips (assessment centres)
Good advice on what to expect and how to perform
http://www.prospects.ac.uk/interview_tips_assessment_centres.htm

● **Jobs.ac.uk**
www.jobs.ac.uk
http://www.jobs.ac.uk/careers-advice/interview-tips/1821/
surviving-the-assessment-centre/
Surviving the Assessment Centre
Suggestions on how to prepare for an assessment centre

● **Kent University Careers and Employability Service**
http://www.kent.ac.uk/careers/selection.htm
Assessment Centres
Good background information

What to do next

Start doing your research on employers that interest you. Find out
how they recruit. Keep in mind the employer perspective as you do
your research.

Getting selected

Contents

Getting selected is the goal of the whole assessment centre and interview process. It can involve passing successfully through a series of recruitment stages and/or making it through to a final job offer.

It can be exhilarating if you know what to expect and how to rev up for each aspect of the selection process used by a particular recruiter. It doesn't have to be an ego-bruising experience.

A good starting point is to understand the different selection processes used by graduate recruiters. Distinct stages of the process act as a filtering system to decide who will go through to the final stage. You need to know how to make it through these qualifying stages. Think of it as getting in training.

Be a recruiter

Recruiters have to sort out the potentially good candidates from the unsuitable or simply hopeless. How would you do this if you were on the recruiting side?

Trawling for potential

This trawling through applications is referred to as 'shortlisting'. Shortlisting is a pretty boring business. Unfortunately, many applicants churn out the same old, same old phrases and make the same old, same old mistakes.

Increasingly, recruiters are testing out a range of ways to make it easier for them to fast-trawl through candidates and yet not miss the candidates with genuine potential.

Methods recruiters use

Take a look at some possible methods used to shortlist applicants.

1. **Online tests:** These will normally be numerical, verbal, personality or situational judgement tests. Your test results give information about your abilities over and above your standard educational qualifications.
2. **Online application form:** This allows a recruiter to see how you present yourself in writing. The recruiter will want to check how you show that you match the job specification.
3. **CV and cover letter:** The CV (curriculum vitae) and letter give basic information about you. Can you show that you are an ideal applicant? You need to shape this information to show how you match the job.
4. **Online challenge:** This could be a timed task where you have to find out something quickly or work out a puzzle. It will reveal your ability to solve a problem and think creatively. It's more common as part of recruitment for the creative industries. This may be for a marketing or advertising or social media role.
5. **Written piece:** You might be required to read something and summarise it or give an opinion on a current issue or a dilemma. It's intended to test your ability to express yourself clearly.
6. **Showreel®/YouTube® clip:** This is more usual for creative film and media professions. You might be expected to be able to present yourself through a video or your own YouTube channel. It will show your ability to 'perform' to an audience and use technology.
7. **10 tweets about yourself:** This is another communication test and requires you to write clearly and concisely. It will reveal your self-knowledge and social media confidence.
8. **Portfolio of work examples:** For design professions, this is very much the norm. These examples should clearly show off your talent. Recruiters will want to access this portfolio online.

9. **Self-selection tool (you decide if you are suitable):** The NHS uses this for its graduate management scheme,[1] and other employers have a version of this. It's a way for a recruiter to help you decide if you are right for the job role before applying.
10. **Leave a message saying why you want the job:** This is a fiendish way of finding out how you come across on the telephone, your research into the job and organisation, and how you express yourself.

The most likely methods

Whilst all of these methods have been used by different recruiters, research into the selection methods of the top 100 graduate employers (High Fliers Research 2014) found the following:[2]

- 94% used an online application form.
- 83% used online aptitude tests.
- 33% used an online self-selection tool.
- 26% asked for a CV and covering letter.
- 24% used a personality questionnaire assessment.

What is certain is that your first encounter with a prospective employer will take place in an online dimension.

"Online promotion continues to be the most popular marketing activity with 96.3% of AGR employers engaging in this ..." (Association of Graduate Recruiters (AGR) 2014).[3]

Some of the less usual methods might seem a bit challenging. If you are wondering how you might handle these, don't worry! This topic will be covered in depth as you go through the book (especially in Chapter 8).

Making the shortlist

The process of application may vary from employer to employer but the essence of what it takes to be shortlisted is fairly obvious. You will need to show the following characteristics to the organisation or company:

- You have a genuine motivation to work there.
- You have developed the skills and attributes it seeks.
- You have taken the trouble to undertake in-depth research into its mission/purpose.

Chapter 2

- You have followed the application process instructions as recommended.

Read what Christine Mabilat from Disney advises.

Employer's view – Christine Mabilat, Director of Employer Brand, Talent Acquisition & Total Rewards at Disneyland® Paris

When we receive an application, there are a great number of things we look for in the candidate.

THE CV – From the outset, it's really important to write a clearly structured and straightforward CV, with your key skills at the top and a statement of what you're looking for.

THE SKILLS – Qualifications and experience are important, but what we look for most of all are excellent interpersonal skills and team spirit, which will help you evolve and develop great working relationships at our company.

Our employer brand tagline is "Making dreams come true is a real job" because each Cast Member is dedicated to providing the best experience possible to our guests. This is why people skills are so important, both towards our visitors and fellow Cast Members. Perhaps you won't be in direct contact with our guests, but your job behind the scenes has an impact on their overall experience at our resort. All Cast Members are part of the show.

THE APPLICATION – INITIAL STAGES – Candidates are invited to create a profile on our website, disneylandparis-casting.com, where they can attach their CV and cover letter. They can either create an unsolicited application or apply directly to a job that interests them. Our recruiters then treat the application and contact the candidate whether his or her profile fits or not. Interviews will follow this stage, then further interviews with departmental managers if the job is quite specific.

If candidates have questions during the initial stages, we encourage them to use our social media platforms where they can post directly onto Facebook®, Twitter® or LinkedIn® for our teams to pick up and answer.

So it's useful to realise how recruiters process your application and also that they are keen to help you to avoid the reject pile. Your CV or application form will be 'scanned' by a human being or by computer software. Your application will be 'sifted' for certain key skills or words or competencies, as laid out in the job specification or on the website careers recruitment page. These specified competencies or attributes are often referred to as 'desirable' or 'essential' criteria.

Desirable and essential criteria

You need to ensure that your application, in any format, will stand out because it 'nails' each and every one of the ideal criteria stated in the specification.

Essential criteria for the job are normally clearly listed in application information. These will be 'absolutes'. Unless you possess these exact qualifications or experience, it is pointless to apply for this role.

Desirable criteria will also be indicated in the application information. The employer is hoping for these extras. If you can show these as well as the essential criteria, you will stand out.

Most companies or organisations provide detailed information about their shortlisting criteria. This will be found as a role profile or person specification or as a list of strengths or competencies associated with the role. It will look something like the abbreviated example of the role profile shown below.

Example: Legal assistant role profile	
Knowledge/experience	**Desirable/Essential (D/E)**
LLB	E
Law clinic voluntary experience	E
Customer/client service	E
Research in law libraries	D
Skills/competencies	
Ability to interact with the general public	E
Ability to provide accountable service	E
Ability to identify specific case law examples, relevant to ongoing cases	D

Chapter 2

Be a 'shortlister'

Imagine an additional tick box final column to this role profile. Shortlisters will read through the CV or application and/or covering letter looking for examples of *each and every* aspect listed on this grid. They will check that examples you give for each skill or competence are genuine and convincing.

The next exercise lets you experience what it is like to review an application. Check it carefully for the key characteristics demanded by the legal assistant job role. You will notice that the applicant has sequenced her statement in the same order as the job specification.

Desirable and essential criteria: Be a shortlister – part 1

1. Consider this section of a candidate's application form.
2. Decide whether the applicant has offered evidence of the relevant criteria.

My recent study for my LLB has allowed me to build my knowledge of family case law so that I have been able to give advice under supervision in a community law clinic.

Without breaching confidentiality, I have recently been involved in a determination for a custody hearing and provided written testimony based on research for the case.

This involved multiple meetings with the client and a court family adviser to build a fruitful relationship with the client and effectively advocate for a client who had recognised communication difficulties.

As a result, I received a written commendation from the solicitor involved and I used this as a re-enactment in a recent moot court as part of my university course.

Be a shortlister – part 2

1. Find a convincing example in the application form statement for each line of the specification.
2. Tick the final column if you think the applicant has proved a match to the job role.

Knowledge/experience	D/E	✓
LLB	D	
Law clinic voluntary experience	E	
Customer/client service	E	
Research in law libraries	D	
Skills/competencies		
Ability to interact with the general public	E	
Ability to provide accountable service	E	
Ability to identify specific case law examples, relevant to ongoing cases	D	

Conclusion The applicant has demonstrated a good match with the essential criteria. She shows that she possesses at least one of the desirable criteria.

Make it easy for the shortlister

You can make it easy for the shortlister to notice each skill or competence example. Try drafting your statements on the application form in the sequence they appear on the specification.

Selection success

Best advice Take the following approach as your guide:

- Know what you can present about yourself to show your suitability for a role (what you have to offer).
- Assess your application rigorously, even ruthlessly.
- Check if you have shown, line by line, that you match the exact details they have provided.
- Check that examples you give are convincing.
- Sequence your examples according to the order shown in the job specification.

Chapter 2

Do this and you will improve your hit rate in terms of getting through to the next stage. To do this in a persuasive way, you will need to know what it is you can offer, by way of Knowledge/Expertise, Skills and Interests. This is a continuation of the self-assessment work you did in Chapter 1.

What you have to offer

All the knowledge of how to get yourself selected is a waste of space if you don't know what you have to offer. You need to analyse yourself and your unique talents. You can then present this to potential graduate employers as evidence of your absolute suitability for their specific roles.

Try some expansive thinking

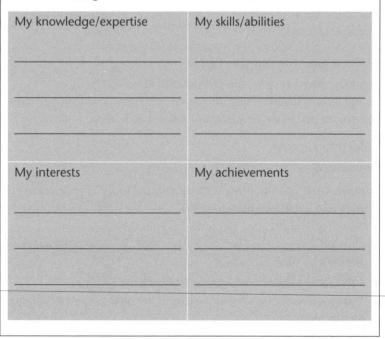

Self-assessment: What you have to offer

1. Note down anything that comes to mind in the four boxes below.
2. Allow yourself to dream a bit, and do not rule anything out.
3. Keep noting things down until you run out of ideas.
4. Show it to three people who know you. Ask them to add their ideas to the grid.

My knowledge/expertise	My skills/abilities
My interests	My achievements

Making sense of it all

Take some time to analyse what you and others have written on the grid.

Think about what you have recorded. Take some time to analyse what it means. Follow this process:

Common themes Notice any patterns that suggest a clear picture of you. Do you agree with what others think of you?

Surprises Consider what any surprises might mean. If more than one person has noted the same thing about you, this might be worth some reflection. It may be that you have a 'blind spot' about yourself, an overlooked talent.

Evidence/examples As you begin to realise your strengths, start to think of tangible examples for each skill, ability or achievement noted. Try to think of one example or piece of evidence that would prove you possess that quality. Make a record of these pieces of evidence.

Keep all this for reference It will be useful for applications and interviews. This is just the start.

Your social media persona

You have embarked on a process of self-knowing. This will prepare you brilliantly for any kind of application process. There's much more to know though. It's time to step out into the digital realm. Graduate recruiters will be using online methods to attract your attention via the company website, social media and job boards (AGR 2014)[3] but it's increasingly common that some kind of social media screening might also take place.

In a CareerBuilder survey, it was found that 'Nearly two in five companies (37%) use social networking sites to research job candidates' (CareerBuilder 2012).[4]

So what will they dig up about you if they research you?

What does your Facebook profile say about you? Are you on LinkedIn? Do you use Instagram? Any social media activity leaves traces or footprints of you that may be accessed through various Internet searches.

This presence is an indicator of how you present yourself to the world and in particular your professional persona. It also gives an indication of your social media savviness. It can be used as a speed selection process by recruiters. It has been known to convince employers as often as it deters them. Sixty-eight per cent of employers in a Reppler 2011[5] survey reported that they hired candidates because of a positive social media presence.

Does the 'you' that has applied to their company match up to the 'you' that is displayed in various social media spaces. So what can be found about you? Is it impressive? It is worth doing a digital reputation check if you are unsure about this. You can use Google Alert[6] or Reppler[7] social media monitoring to do this.

Most importantly, expect that recruiters might check and assess your digital presence, in particular how you are using social media. Here's a quick way to check your social media presence. It's often referred to as 'vanity googling'.

Vanity googling

Firstly, think of three people you know and google them. What comes up? Anything? Is it complimentary and positive? In fact, whatever is out there about a person should be complimentary and complementary. It should show them in the best possible way (complimentary) and it should add and cross-reference consistently with all their other digital activity (complementary).

Found nothing about your three people?

They don't exist on Google. This might be problematic. Guess! Why might this be a problem? There may be many reasons for non-appearance in a Google search. Your selected person might be someone who

- has a really common name or even a similar name to a celebrity;
- is an 'anti–social media' person;
- is a private person who enjoys non-digital activities; or
- is in the early stages of life or a career.

There could be many other reasons of course. Being invisible on Google could actually be the sign of a highly enlightened person who chooses not to conform.

The problematic element

There are two main problems for someone who is actively seeking a brilliant career.

Firstly, the damage effect If there is a negative impression on social media, this could act as a deterrent to prospective employers. Inattention to what is revealed about you (or your lack of awareness of this), might prevent a recruiter from shortlisting you. In the Reppler research[8] 47% of the surveyed hiring professionals (300 in total) reported that they would check an applicant's social media profile after receiving his or her application. It would be a pity to be rejected at the application stage.

Secondly, the dinosaur effect If you are studiously disengaged with all social media platforms, this reluctance might give the impression of a fervent 'flat earth' believer who cannot accept progress. This second effect is very much about an impression. It is not necessarily the truth, but it may be perceived in a negative light. Most of the application process is about impressions you create. True self-awareness is the ability to notice impressions that you give and control perceptions that others form about you.

Your social media story

Now do the same for yourself, ideally from a strange computer that you do not usually use. It's likely that you'll be directed through Google to your Facebook or LinkedIn page. How do you come across? Is it a true and impressive representation?

See yourself as others will see you. Aim to judge yourself in a cold and neutral way. How does this view of you match up with your findings from that previous self-assessment activity? Think of all of this as your very own social media career story.

It's highly advisable that you engage with social media in whatever way feels right for you. You should see yourself in charge of this and determine what you want to be revealed there. Think of it as another way that you can demonstrate your own career and personal motivations.

Chapter 2

Getting selected via social media

Align your profiles You have to tell a consistent and positive story about yourself. Make sure that your headline statements (the descriptor lines under your name) on all profiles match up.

Check your settings Whether it is Twitter, LinkedIn, Facebook, Instagram, Pinterest or some other blog platform or portfolio space, check and adjust your privacy settings. Be warned: social media background checks will be used by some employers.

Make yourself findable Ensure that you are findable due to appropriate and commendable social media activity (rather than endless commentary about trivial issues).

Be smart about what you put out there An ill-advised rant in your digital profile can be destructive and even sabotage your career. Be aware of the impact of what you post.

An additional part of the online environment, often the very first stage of the recruitment process, involves selection or rejection by way of online tests.

Online selection tests

Performing well in these tests

The process of applying for graduate jobs can often seem really convoluted. It can seem as if the application and selection process is a series of roadblocks and diversions designed to frustrate and demotivate applicants. Online tests seem like just another fiendish difficulty placed in an applicant's way.

This is very much the applicant perspective and a genuine response to how it may feel. The good news is that you can prepare and practise for these tests, so there is no need to dread them.

Remember that employers use tests to

- identify talent in applicants; and
- save time in the selection and recruitment process.

Online tests are a really quick and effective way for them to assess potential and reduce the number of applicants to a manageable shortlist. These tests are often referred to as psychometric tests. They are quite different from tests or exams you might have experienced. Psychometric tests are created by occupational psychologists. They are designed to be accurate in predicting potential ability and behaviour. (There is more about psychometrics in Chapters 3, 4 and 5).

Most online tests are timed aptitude or ability tests. There will be specific right or wrong answers for the ability test questions. Typically, you might be tested with 20 questions in 20 minutes or 30 questions in 30 minutes. Many offer multiple-choice answers. Expect to encounter these common ability test types in the early application stages:

Numerical tests
These tests focus on basic arithmetic (addition, multiplication, percentages and fractions) and are testing your ability to handle numbers.

Numerical reasoning tests
These go a stage further and may ask you to interpret data from a table or chart.

Verbal tests
These may test your vocabulary, spelling, punctuation or basic understanding of a passage of text.

Verbal reasoning or logical reasoning tests
These are like a comprehension test, requiring you to read and understand a passage and answer questions or agree/disagree with statements.

Speed testing

Here are some purposely easy examples of the kind of questions found in some of these tests. This is a just a fun way for you to experience them. Set a timer to 5 minutes. There are four example questions. Aim to get through them all within the 5-minute deadline. Your time starts now.

Numerical test	
Fill in the missing number in the mathematical equation.	
1. $987 = 357 + ?$	1. _____
2. $53 \times 7 - ? = 318$	2. _____
3. $144 - 60 = ?$	3. _____

Numerical reasoning test: Social media use by families

Look at the graph and answer the questions below.

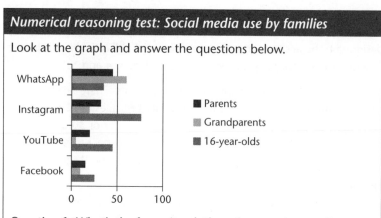

Question 1: What's the favourite platform for grandparents?
Question 2: What's the favourite platform for parents?
Question 3: What's the favourite platform for teenagers?
Question 4: What's the most used platform by all three groups?

Question 1	1. _____
Question 2	2. _____
Question 3	3. _____
Question 4	4. _____

Verbal test

Which sentence has the correct spelling of 'stationary'?	Put 'Right' or Wrong' on the corresponding lines below.
Sentence 1: She went to the post office to buy some stationary.	1. _____
Sentence 2: The postman's van was stationary as he emptied the postbox.	2. _____

Verbal reasoning or logical reasoning test

Read the passages below.

Decide whether the statements are True or False.

Many graduates find themselves underemployed after university. They need to be earning so often take the first job they see or otherwise carry on in a part-time job. Only 8.9% of graduates are unemployed 6 months after leaving university. The graduates who have gained relevant work experience are more likely to gain graduate-level roles.

Statement 1: Graduates don't plan for life after university.

Statement 2: Most graduates gain work within 6 months of leaving university.

Statement 3: Relevant work experience is significant in helping students to become successful working graduates.

True statement(s)   _____

False statement(s)   _____

So how did you find these examples? How did you cope with the speed element? Even with relatively easy questions, the time aspect may cause a candidate to panic. Remember that as a general rule, it is best to stick to no more than a minute per question, as a rough guide. Generally, the time will only start when you have read the instructions. There will be an on-screen prompt telling you how many questions you have answered and indicating the time that is remaining.

These were just a gentle taster of the tests you will come across. The real ones are tougher and will challenge you with a sequence of increasingly difficult questions. These are not tests that you can take without some preparation and practice. Chapters 3, 4 and 5 will give you more in-depth help with psychometrics and directions to the practice versions which the test publishers make available. You *will* be ready to be tested.

Develop your speed at tests

Practice obviously helps, but the timed aspect of most online tests adds to the pressure to perform well. Some applicants recommend a resource for numerical tests which allows you to build up your speed and accuracy. Take a look at Calculation Rankings (www.calculationrankings.com/game) and it might help tap into your competitive streak.

It's also useful to have strategies to deal with questions. For example, with multiple-choice questions you can often identify the wrong answers quickly, eliminate them and arrive at the right one. For further coping strategies, see Chapters 4 and 5.

Answers to tests

Find out how you did.

Numerical test

Fill in the missing number in the mathematical equation

$987 = 357 + 630$

$53 \times 7 - 53 = 318$

$144 - 60 = 84$

Numerical reasoning test

Grandparents and parents like WhatsApp best.

Teenagers like Instagram best.

Most used platform – WhatsApp.

Verbal test

Which sentence has the right spelling of 'stationary'?

The correct use and spelling of 'stationary' was in Sentence 2.

Verbal reasoning or logical reasoning test

Statement 1: Graduates don't plan for life after university.
False

Statement 2: Most graduates gain work within 6 months of leaving university. *True*

Statement 3: Relevant work experience is significant in helping students to become successful working graduates.
True

Test battering

Don't expect to be subjected to every single type of test. The online tests will be based on the job role. Numerical tests are used more for business and finance roles. Verbal tests are used for roles where written communication is important. Many employers use what is called a 'battery' of tests, typically two or three.

Test location

Remember you will probably be doing these tests at home or ideally in some private computer space. You will need to concentrate and give yourself the best chance to perform well.

Be careful to ensure that you are in a quiet environment without distractions and that you have a pen and paper and registration details (if they have asked you to register) close by. Check whether you will be allowed to use a calculator. In addition, make sure you have a good Internet connection and a computer or device that will not fail you. Have a glass of water to hand, and make sure you have been to the toilet beforehand. Test sessions can be long (1 hour typically).

So here are a few ideas to give you the best chance of doing well:

Practise on the practice tests Good recruitment schemes will direct you to the relevant practice tests. The tests will be more familiar that way.

Find a test buddy Research and try out tests with a friend who is good at maths and/or English. Work out strategies to help you deal with questions.

Practise numeracy without a calculator Get yourself used to making quick calculations in your head. You may be allowed to use calculators for certain tests, but your mental ability needs to speed up.

The overall score counts Keep going, and avoid getting bogged down on one question. If you are unsure and time is flying, mark your 'best guess' choice and move on.

Resilience tactics

It can feel like a knockout competition. It can be demoralising to be part of such an intensely competitive process. However, successful applicants have the ability to focus on their ultimate goals and persevere, despite setbacks. You will need grit and resilience. Resilience is the ability to bounce back from adversity. Angela Duckworth describes grit as 'the tendency to sustain interest in and effort towards very long-term goals'.[9]

These qualities of grit and resilience are vital in the selection process. It may seem like an endurance test. You will not be the only one who gets it wrong at times. Adversity is the training ground for grit and resilience. You can try *Angela Duckworth's Grit Test* to give you an idea of your personal grit score.[10] The good news is that with the right attitude, you can become better at dealing with these challenging first stages.

Finally, remember that you are not the only one who will be fighting your way through the selection process. Most applicants scream, wail, curse a bit and yet many get through it all with preparation and determination.

Chapter 2

Summary of key points

Know what you have to offer: Be ready to showcase your talents, skills and abilities in your application through clear examples.
Make the shortlist: Do this by rigorously showing how you match the criteria of the job specification.
Be ready for online tests: Check what tests will be used and practise them to develop speed and accuracy.
Build up your grit and resilience: Stay focused on your goals and bounce back if you fail.

Find out more

The following websites contain information on recruitment and selection processes:

- **Graduate Recruitment Bureau**
  http://employers.grb.uk.com/selection-methods
  Good advice from the employer's perspective.

- **University of Kent Careers and Employability Service**
  http://www.kent.ac.uk/careers/selection.htm
  Read through the explanations of typical selection methods.
- **Kenexa Practice Online Tests**
  http://www.psl.com/practice/
  Have a go at numerical and verbal tests.

What to do next

Get in training by taking a look at the practice tests and the examples.
Test yourself. Build up speed. Try out Calculation Rankings:
www.calculationrankings.com/game

Chapter 5

Psychometrics and assessment day tests

Contents

The whole process of recruitment is about assessment of applicants. Two-thirds of employers use an assessment centre process to recruit staff, particularly graduates and managers (Personnel Today 2011)[1].

Recruiters use various methods to get to know applicants, judging who is best for their purposes. For most applicants, the initial stages will be online and will include an application form and some online tests. The whole process is, in fact, a prolonged testing of applicants.

The most recent research into the top 100 graduate employers (High Fliers 2014)[2] indicates that online applications are the norm (94% of recruiters in the High Fliers research). Prior to a selection/assessment day, you will have made a successful online application, which will have included some online tests.

You can be justifiably pleased that you have passed the first-stage tests. This is sometimes signified by a recruitment name change. You go from being an 'applicant' to a 'candidate'. You have improved your chance of success significantly.

As a reward for your success so far, you may find yourself tested again. This time you'll find yourself sitting in a room with other candidates, being subjected to tests in formal exam conditions.

So how's this different?

Well, the online test environment is private, almost secret. The assessment day testing is more public. It is just one aspect of the assessment day. It can seem tense enough without a battery of psychometric question papers. So why will you encounter more psychometric tests?

Why psychometrics?

The word 'psychometric' means 'measure of the mind'. A psychometric assessment or test is designed to find out how your mind works and its capability. That's the simple way of thinking about psychometric tests.

You've started to know something about these tests by finding out about the online test versions. Having passed an online test, you might still have to replicate this performance through a repeat test experience on an assessment day. Psychometric tests on the assessment day often go further than the online versions. You will need to move up a gear and prepare for all the versions of tests you might encounter.

What tests reveal

In some ways, the use of psychometric tests is just another way for an employer to get to know you. Applicants can claim to possess all kinds of abilities and attributes on application forms and CVs. You could say that you have amazing powers of deduction, for example. You could give a convincing example of how you have used this power. It could all be fiction. You could be talking a good talk. In an online test, an applicant might not have actually taken the test. She might have persuaded a gifted friend to do the test for her. Assessment day tests are backup insurance for employers. By testing you on the day, they know it is you who has taken the assessment. The scores are an accurate representation of your abilities or attributes *on that day*.

When to expect them

You may encounter them at either of these two stages:

- At a first-stage event as a 'qualifier' for the main assessment centre day.
- As part of the assessment day.

Chapter 3

Test dynamics

Your mental state

For many applicants, just the word 'test' generates negative memories. This negative thinking mind-state is not the best preparation. It may actually sabotage your performance. It's useful to become aware of this tendency so you can prevent it.

Think back to test situations you have experienced. This could be your driving theory test, medical or veterinary school tests (BMAT or UKCAT) or school exams. What were you thinking prior to these tests? The next exercise will help you be aware of your own mental state before a test.

Self-assessment: Your test mind-state

Note down anything that comes to mind in the four boxes below.

Memories of previous tests	Thoughts about tests

Feelings when confronted with tests	Tests I like

This exercise is intended to raise your awareness of the habitual thoughts and feelings you experience when confronted by tests. Take a moment to assess yourself. Do you have a balanced view of tests, or is your mind-state predominately gloomy about them? It's time to work on that mind-state.

Priming your thinking

If your memories, thoughts and feelings about tests are predominantly negative, it's likely that your test performance will be under par. That negative mind-state can induce a condition of 'learned helplessness'[3] which Martin Seligman believes is incapacitating. It could mean that you approach a test expecting to fail. You are actually priming your mind to fail.

The good news is that you can change your thinking by 'priming' your mind. Imagine for just a moment that you are a really clever professor. If you were that stereotype, how would you do in a test? Thinking from that mind-state, you would expect to do really well in a test. It turns out that making yourself 'think about' being smart can actually improve your performance in a test. There's a link between your perception of your intelligence and your performance. It seems mad, but research from the Netherlands tested this out with groups of students.[4] Those that *imagined* themselves as clever prior to sitting a test actually did better. This focused, priming activity works at a subconscious level. Even the mental activity of recalling previous, minor successes or achievements can help you ready your mind for a testing challenge. So try out this change of mind-state prior to a test. Use your imagination to prime your mind for intelligence.

Tests you like

In the fourth box on the self-assessment exercise, what did you write in 'Tests I like'? The strange thing is that often people say they hate tests and forget that there are certain tests they like. You might dislike numerical tests but like crosswords or sudoku. You might dislike verbal tests but like word searches or puzzles.

If you can shift your attention slightly to the kind of tests you like, you might discover a better focus for approaching tests.

Best advice

Take these steps to improve and rev up your overall test performance.

Your frame of mind Become aware of your own thought patterns and redirect them through consciously focusing on positive thoughts, feelings and memories.

Find out more about tests Knowing what to expect, including the purpose of each type of test, can really help your overall performance.

For most applicants, the next most useful strategy is to understand the types of tests and get familiar with them through trying them on for size.

Understanding tests

More and more recruiters are using psychometric tests at some stage of the recruitment process. Of 200 large employers interviewed by the Association of Graduate Recruiters (AGR), 67% were using some kind of psychometric assessment.[5] You might not be able to avoid them.

> 67% of employers are using psychometric tests (AGR 2013).

Tests are 'owned' by particular organisations and are administered by trained professionals (occupational psychologists or registered test users). Different test publishers, such as SHL, Kenexa, TalentQ, Cubiks and Saville Consulting, produce them. The most common ones have been well researched. They are deemed to have high 'predictive validity'. That means they are reliable in assessing what they claim to assess.

Practice tests

You will be directed by a recruiter to practice test versions, which are especially useful in demystifying the whole test process. There are three types of practice tests:

- **General sample tests** which are recommended by the employer and test publisher.
- **Worked examples** of test questions, which allow you to have a go, check your answer and learn the best way to get to the result.
- **A pre-test example question** with an answer at the beginning of the actual test, which allows you to be familiar with the type of test questions just before you start the test for real.

Even though you know something about tests from the online test examples in Chapter 2, there's a great deal more to know.

The most common tests

There are so many tests used by recruiters, but they tend to fall into three main categories. These are the most common ones.

Most common psychometric tests	
Ability or aptitude tests	These test numerical, verbal and spatial aptitudes. (These can be online – see Chapter 2.)
Critical thinking or situational judgement tests	These assess your ability to reason and make good judgements.
Personality tests	These aim to discover your personal qualities, your motivation style and the way you respond to different situations or challenges.

You are likely to encounter more than one type of test on an assessment day. The selected tests will be specifically aligned to the requirements of the job role. For example, in a research/policy officer role, verbal and critical thinking skills will be important. In a banking role, verbal and numerical skills will be needed. Specific ability tests for these roles will help an employer know how capable an applicant is.

Ability tests

You may have encountered ability tests as part of the online selection process. These tests are designed to assess your actual aptitude in a number of specific areas. Typically, they test your capacity for numerical, verbal or spatial skills. Variations on these themes have 'reasoning' tagged on to their titles. A verbal reasoning test goes further than basic knowledge of spellings, grammar and words. It assesses how you work out the meaning of a passage of text. Similarly, numerical reasoning tests require you to puzzle out the meanings from a graph or chart.

The right answer

The key thing about these types of tests is that there *is* a right or wrong answer for each question. Most importantly, be aware of the following issues:

- You will be scored on the number of right answers so accuracy *and* speed matter.
- Many tests are based on multiple-choice or true/false questions so, if in doubt, make a best guess.

- Getting stuck on one question loses you time so move on if necessary and go back at the end if you have time (if it allows you to do so).
- There will be more questions than an average applicant can complete in the time allotted.
- Questions often increase in difficulty as you go through the test.

Time pressures

The time factor is trying. These tests take place in timed, exam-like conditions. It is you against the clock. You have to get the right balance between speed and accuracy. However, it's a real mistake to let the time factor take over your thinking. Your focus should be on each question, allowing yourself to concentrate on what it is demanding of you.

> Decide quickly how long you can spend on each question. Typically, you may have a minute per question.

Take a measured approach by:

- Reading the question thoroughly
- Checking that you understand it
- Finding the quickest way to the answer (which might be from a multiple-choice selection).

Worked examples

All the main test publishers recommend their practice tests. These give you an idea of what to expect and allow you to practise and speed up. Often, there are worked examples with answers in the practice tests to help you know what to expect. The actual assessment centre day tests also generally show a worked example at the beginning of each test.

Scoring for tests

The employer has decided the abilities required for the job. The test provider (who designed the test) will have piloted the test with a particular group (probably made up of previous successful candidates). The usual result or score of this group of successful candidates will be the benchmark used. You are being measured against this group's typical score.

At an assessment centre, you might not necessarily be in direct competition with other candidates who are there on the day. Everyone could pass if they achieve the required score. So what kind of ability tests do different employers use? It's useful to know what to expect according to the type of employer and the job role. Here are some examples:

Accountancy and banking You can expect numerical and verbal ability tests and situational judgement tests.

Computer technology You will be tested through a computer aptitude test, which assesses your logical reasoning and ability to process information quickly.

Construction and engineering It is usual to be assessed via numerical, verbal and spatial tests.

Health This will be dependent on job role, but for graduate roles in the NHS, verbal and/or numerical reasoning and situational judgement tests are used.

Human resources Critical thinking and situational judgement tests may be used.

Law Critical thinking exercises are the most common. Numerical and verbal tests may also be used.

Media Predominantly verbal, critical thinking and situational judgement tests or video scenarios will be used.

Social care Usually verbal and numerical reasoning and situational judgement tests will be used.

Teaching Professional skills tests in literacy and numeracy are the standard entry assessment for teacher training[6] (postgraduate and undergraduate).

Ability test examples

Here are some lightweight examples of ability tests to give you an idea.

Numerical test
What is the next number in the sequence? 25 50 75 125

Numerical reasoning test

Read the chart and answer the questions below.

Average daily intake of sugar in grams.

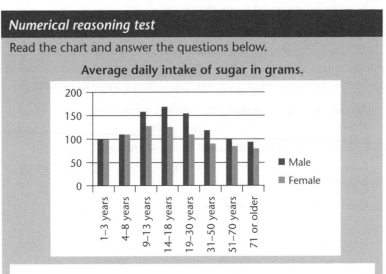

1. What is the average consumption of sugar by males of all ages?
2. What is the average consumption of sugar by females of all ages?
3. What is the overall average consumption, male and female together?
4. One hundred and ten grams is equivalent to 26 teaspoons. How many teaspoons is the average 19-year-old male consuming?

Answer 1	1. _____
Answer 2	2. _____
Answer 3	3. _____
Answer 4	4. _____

Verbal test

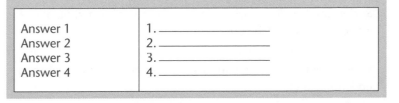

Select the three words from the list below which are closest to the word in the box.

Quirky

Sardonic Amusing Peculiar Unusual Normal Original Idiosyncratic

_____

_____

_____

Non-verbal or spatial reasoning test

Decide the next shape in the sequence from the shapes below.

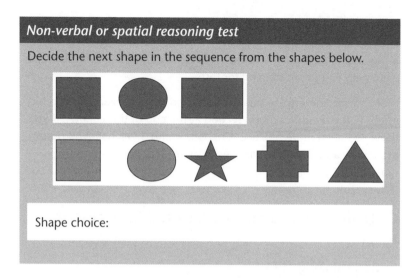

Shape choice:

Feedback from tests: Answers

Numerical
Next number in sequence would be 175 (as it is beginning to jump in 50s).

Numerical reasoning
1. 125 grams
2. 105 grams
3. 115 grams
4. 35 teaspoons

Verbal
Quirky is closer to Original, Unusual and Idiosyncratic.

Non-verbal and spatial tests
The next shape would be a triangle (the missing geometric shape).

So how did you find these examples?

Test panics

If you found these relatively easy, then that is a good start. If these examples have caused you to panic, breathe and remember this:

Chapter 3

- These tests are just strange and unfamiliar to you.
- You can improve your speed and confidence through practice.
- You can check out the worked examples offered by test publishers to help you get in training for tests.

More advice and links to practice tests and worked examples can be found in the 'Find out more' section at the end of this chapter. If you think you need more practice, Chapters 4 and 5 will help you refresh these skills and develop strategies to perform at your best in these types of tests.

Critical thinking and situational judgement tests

Critical thinking (CT)

You've probably come across the term 'critical thinking'. You've probably used this in your studies. The term 'critical thinking' can mean many things but for assessment centre purposes, think of it as a way of:

- Examining a situation from multiple angles.
- Weighing up and making judgement.
- Avoiding black and white or single-track thinking.
- Demonstrating an ability to seek innovative solutions.

The key aspect to note is that critical thinking is not just about being negative. It is about balanced thinking and judgements. For these tests, you will be presented with scenarios which might be in video form or as written statements. You will be asked to determine assumptions or conclusions that can be drawn from each scenario.

Critical thinking and situational judgement tests are in some ways an extension of the verbal/logical reasoning type tests (see Chapter 2 online test examples).

Critical thinking tests require you to be aware of assumptions you have made based on information provided. Often without realising it, you may have taken something for granted as 'true' within a particular statement. Try the next example.

Critical thinking test

1. Read the following extract.
2. Pick the statement which is a reasonable assumption based on this extract.

> People in a typical family living together spend 35 minutes a day shouting at each other, a poll of couples with children showed last week.
>
> It found that 60% of families argue at least once a day. The shouting lasts for an hour or more in 30% of homes, rising to 40% in families with more than one child (Daily Yawn 2012).

Statement 1: Children cause arguments.
Statement 2: Big families argue for longer.
Statement 3: Couples without children argue less.

The reasonable assumption:

_____

Situational judgement tests (SJT)

Imagine the kind of typical work situations you might encounter in a particular job role. These are common challenging situations where you might be tested and find that you really have to think fast. Situational judgement tests are simulations of these typical scenarios. Recruiters want to know how you will deal with them. They might be part of the online assessment phase or the actual assessment day. The next example will give you an idea. You will be expected to select your considered course of action.

Situational judgement test

Read the passage below. Pick a course of action.

> It is a busy lunchtime. A customer who has waited some time arrives at the counter. She wants to cash a cheque for £300. The payee name is hard to read. She offers some ID, but you are not sure if it is a valid cheque.

> **What do you do?**
> 1. You ask her to take a seat and wait. You call for help.
> 2. You ask her to ask the payer to rewrite the cheque, as it is indecipherable.
> 3. You suggest that she asks the payer to arrange a bank transfer of the money online, as this will take less time.
> 4. You explain the problem. You suggest that the cheque needs to be resubmitted at a later date, with a clearly written Payee box.
>
> Course of action: ————————————————

Critical thinking and situational judgement feedback

How did you do with these test examples?

In the **critical thinking test**, the only halfway reasonable assumption was Statement 2. Even that was subject to some uncertainty. The problem with these critical thinking tests is that as the reader of the passage, you can be tempted to let your own opinions on the topic get in the way. Follow this process:

- Fix yourself in an objective, neutral frame of mind at the start.
- Read statements carefully and thoroughly, but work quickly as well.
- Ask yourself whether each one is true or false or a misrepresentation of the facts *as given in the text*.
- Decide if anything can be assumed (not completely substantiated, but a likely supposition).

As a general rule, the well-known tests such as the Watson-Glaser SJT test offer plenty of preparation advice with practice questions and answers to help you know that you are on the right track.

In the **situational judgement test**, the most probable courses of action would be no. 3 or no. 4. Judgements can be less fixed and absolute, but they generally involve an empathic and assertive response (the perfect combination). More test practice and examples can be found in Chapters 4 and 5.

Personality tests are used as a follow-up to ability tests because they provide additional information on an applicant's motivation, values and behaviour. Most companies do not rely on the results of a personality test alone; it is just one part of the assessment of an applicant.

Personality tests

Self-reporting

Most personality tests are self-reporting. What that means is that you decide what to reveal (dependent on how much you know about yourself). You will be prompted to agree or disagree or give a true/false response to set statements.

> Quizmaster asks contestant
> 'And what is your specialist subject?'
> Contestant says 'My specialist subject is me'.

This is why strong self-awareness is so important. Often the test will contain banks of statements, which can be similar or conflicting. You have to be able to make a decision quickly between these statements. Dithering will suggest you lack self-awareness. Think of it this way: Imagine you are a contestant on some TV quiz. Your specialist subject is … you. How would you do?

Personality test examples

A personality test is aimed at uncovering whether applicants have the qualities, behaviours or attitudes required for a particular type of job role.

These required characteristics will have been decided by research into the psychological profiles of previous successful employees or applicants. You will not know exactly the type of person a company has in mind (although you may be able to guess at this). It may be detailed in the person specification for the role. You will be asked to respond to a set of statements. There will be a number of responses to each statement. You will have to pick one. The responses will be presented something like this:

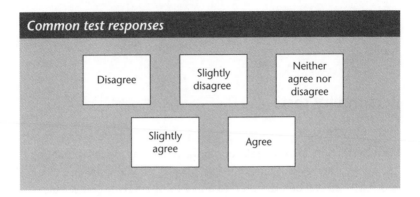

Common test responses

It's a mistake to over-analyse the statements. There will be so many questions/statements to rate in this way. They will look for consistency in your answers. Playing safe and going for the midpoint on the scale is not recommended unless that really feels accurate for you. Sometimes this midpoint 'safe' answer is not offered at all. You may feel forced to make a choice.

Have a go at the following short examples.

Personality test 1: Statements

1. Read the following statements.
2. Decide your response to each statement from the selection below.

Disagree	Slightly disagree	Slightly agree	Agree

Everyone needs to contribute in a team.
Someone has to take the lead in a team.
Large teams are not productive.
Quiet people don't contribute much to a team.

Personality test 2: Statements

1. Read the following statements.
2. Put an 'M' against those that are most like you.
3. Put an 'L' against those that are least like you.

I like to think on my feet.
I work best on my own.
I like to plan and prepare carefully.
I like to work with others.

No right or wrong answers

Whichever way you answered in the two tests, this should be a true representation of you. There are no specific right or wrong answers. The recruiter will select candidates who respond in line with the profile of the ideal person they wish to recruit.

In the second test, for example, there is no real sense of the 'right' answer because it will depend on the job role. Someone who puts an 'M' against Statement 3 may be suited to a tax consultant or an actuarial role. Someone who puts 'M' against Statements 1 and 4 may suit a fast-moving, event-management environment. Someone who puts an 'M' against Statement 2 might suit a research role.

The tests attempt to assess your default behaviour in different situations and your preferred way of doing things. You cannot fix these or create an alternative persona. Aim to be authentically yourself. That's the best approach with personality tests. It can ease the pressure and allow you to perform better.

The OCEAN experience

You may come across a personality test based on what is often referred to as the 'Big 5' personality dimensions. This is often shown as the mnemonic OCEAN (developed by Digman 1990).[7]

Personality dimensions: OCEAN	
O	Openness (to experience and to others)
C	Conscientiousness (how you apply yourself to work or projects)
E	Extroversion (how you can be outgoing)
A	Agreeableness (how you connect with others)
N	Neuroticism (how you manage your nerves and the tendency to worry)

It's really useful to assess yourself against these dimensions, as it builds up self-awareness. How would you rate your openness? How would you rate your agreeableness? It's also a good preparation for personality tests that use the OCEAN framework for their statements (for example SHL's OPQ).

Using the following table, briefly rate yourself on a score of between 1 and 5 for each of these characteristics.

If you believe you are very conscientious, you might give yourself a 4 or a 5. If you think you have a tendency to get stressed, you might give yourself a 1 on the neuroticism dimension. If you manage your nerves well, you might rate yourself at 5. A rating of 5 suggests you are strong in this area. A rating of 1 suggests an area of weakness.

Chapter 3

Self-assessment: OCEAN rating

1. Rate yourself on each dimension.

		Rating 1–5
O	Openness	
C	Conscientiousness	
E	Extroversion	
A	Agreeableness	
N	Neuroticism	

This is just a self-awareness-raising exercise to allow you to see yourself based on these dimensions. Remember, different employers will require different characteristics. An employer might want a high score in conscientiousness, but not on extroversion. It will always depend on the job role.

Common personality tests

The following are the most common personality tests used by employers:

- MBTI® (Myers-Briggs Type Indicator®)
- CIPQ (Cubiks In-Depth Personality Questionnaire, based on the recognised 'Big 5' personality dimensions)
- OPQ (Occupational Personality Questionnaire)
- 16PF® (assessment of 16 personality factors).

Finally, as these tests are about your considered responses, there are generally no time limits.

Dealing with tests

The best approach

Some tests are like a return to primary school tests. Some are more complex. Practice tests are available and are the best way to rev up your thinking, speed and accuracy. Think of it like a footballer's match fitness. You have to train.

Due consideration for disability

Recruiters are required by law to make reasonable adjustments in case of disability and other protected factors. If you, by reason of a particular disability, need special consideration, you need to let the recruiter know in advance so special arrangements can be made. You can learn more about this by checking the British Psychological Society guidelines.[8]

Now read the advice of an occupational psychologist.

My Advice – Eileen Cunningham, chartered occupational psychologist

Begin with a 'can do' attitude, and remember that although you may find the assessments challenging and you might not finish, other people will feel the same. Work as quickly as you can, but not so quickly that you make mistakes.

Read instructions thoroughly, and don't be tempted to skip practice questions or assume that you know how to do a particular test. If you know the time limit and the number of questions, you can make a quick mental calculation of how much time to spend on each one. Check whether you will lose marks for incorrect answers.

Some organisations may give feedback, so it is always worth asking – you might have done a lot better than you thought, and even if you haven't it can give you pointers for further development.

Summary of best advice

Find the practice tests: Search for examples from the main test publishers (see 'Find out more' section) and check what tests will be used by your preferred recruiters.

Test out the tests: Have a go at a good range of practice tests, and determine your strengths and weaknesses.

Check the worked examples: For those that you find tough, make use of the worked examples.

Immerse yourself in tests: Take a sample test every day for 2 weeks. Get used to them.

Re-activate your primary school brain: Borrow/buy refresher arithmetic and comprehension books and work through some of the examples.

Get into word games and mental puzzles: Keep your brain in training.

Check instructions given by the recruiter: Listen carefully and/ or read through the instructions with full concentration.

Best guess: If you are struggling and it is a multiple choice, go for a considered 'best guess' estimate.

Find out more

- **Kent University Careers Service**
  http://www.kent.ac.uk/careers/psychotests.htm
  There are really good examples of tests on this website.

- **Psychometric Success**
  http://www.psychometric-success.com/
  Downloadable e-book.

- **SHL Direct – practice tests**
  www.shldirect.com/en/practice-tests

- **Cubiks – practice tests**
  http://practicetests.cubiks.com

- **Watson Glaser Practice Test** (critical thinking)
  http://www.assessmentday.co.uk/watson-glaser-critical-thinking
  .htm

- **OPP – personality tests**
  http://www.opp.com/
  Read about MBTI® and the 16PF®.

What to do next

Get in training. Immerse yourself in different kinds of tests. Follow this up with Chapters 4 and 5, where you will have the chance to refresh your skills and learn the best tactics to perform successfully at tests.

Chapter **4**

Numerical ability assessment:

Contents

Love them or loathe them, numerical ability assessments are an increasingly popular selection tool. There is a very good chance that you will encounter them as part of the assessment process.

This chapter will help you feel more calm, competent and confident about the kinds of tests you may face. If you are already brilliant with numbers, you still need to know about some of the practical things that could help give you the edge.

Numerical ability tests can assess your ability to:

- Identify the most relevant information from a mass of data.
- Perform basic arithmetic functions.
- Interpret statistics, tables and charts.
- Solve a real-life problem involving quantities or costs.
- Do all of the above quickly and accurately.

Chapter 3 gave you a broad idea of what to expect from psychometric assessments. Now we will focus on specific examples and show you, step by step, the skills and strategies which will help you to succeed. This chapter will help you to develop these skills and to feel calm and confident.

Confidence with numbers

If you are a person who thinks, "I couldn't do maths at school; I am no good with numbers" then think again. In practice, these assessments test a mixture of natural ability and things you have learnt. And can learn. Reflect upon your beliefs about numeracy and challenge your assumptions. This will help you to approach the assessment in a positive frame of mind.

Maths myths: True or false?

1. Read the following statements.
2. Put a 'T' against those you think are true.
3. Put an 'F' against those you think are false.

	T/F
You have to get all the answers right in numerical assessments.	
Numeracy is useful in everyday life.	
Practice makes perfect.	
You can either do maths or you can't.	

How did you find this? What do you notice about your beliefs? Now examine each statement and how it relates to your thinking about maths and how you view your potential.

You have to get all the answers right False. The pass mark might actually be lower than you think. You may even get more wrong than right and still get through. Assessments can often be used as a sift to check that you have a functional level of ability rather than to choose the candidate with the top marks. Your score will be compared with the results of thousands of other people. You may need to do better than at least 40% of those other people. This will, of course, depend upon the job and the level of numeracy required. Actuarial careers will require an exceedingly high level of numeracy, whereas the 'pass mark' may be lower for other roles which may prioritise verbal skills.

Numeracy is useful in everyday life True. You already use numbers every day, for example:

- Every time you buy something.
- Working out how much you would save in a 10% off sale.

- Understanding your mobile phone contract.
- Adding up scores in a game of darts.
- Splitting shared household bills fairly.

Moreover, understanding numbers can have a significant impact upon your future health and happiness. Effectively calculating risks, estimating the impact of mortgage rate rises and managing your money will help your life run smoothly.

Practice makes perfect False. There is undeniably some truth in this old adage. Merely practising over and over again can be pointless, though. It could actually impair your performance if you just keep getting better at making mistakes. So how can you make it work? Well, there are two additional things you need in order to improve. First of all, you need feedback on what you are doing wrong and how to do it right. Secondly, you need to reflect upon your practice and learn from the experience. You can then apply this learning the next time you take a test.

Whilst practice doesn't necessarily make perfect, refreshing your knowledge of some of the basic ways of working with numbers will help you to perform better.

You can either do maths or you can't False. Evidence from fields such as neuroscience and social research suggest that ability and 'intelligence' are not as fixed as once was thought.[1]

Although often used interchangeably, 'mathematical aptitude' and 'numerical ability' are slightly different concepts. Maths teaches you to apply tried and tested processes and theories to numbers. Numerical ability is a more 'common sense' ability to understand and interpret numbers. It shouldn't require expert knowledge.

So even if you found maths hard at school, you can be good at numeracy. What's more, if you believe that you only have a limited amount of ability you will probably prove yourself right!

Natural ability vs. learned ability

Some people do seem to be better at maths than others. There are a number of complex factors which influence this. However, there is increasing evidence that such cognitive skills are a result of practice and motivation to learn, rather than simply innate talents. Mihaly Csikszentmihalyi[2] is an expert on what brings out the best in people.

He suggests that 'talented teenagers' don't necessarily have special abilities. They work harder and practise more. In neuroscience, the study of the brain, there is increasing evidence to suggest that your ability is less fixed than you might think. This is very reassuring news.

Some people think that males are better at maths than females. However, differences in ability are most likely to be a result of environmental factors rather than innate ability. For example, competitiveness, the expectations and encouragement of teachers, parents and society or gender stereotypes may significantly affect someone's attainment level in maths.

So there may be people who can whizz through a numerical assessment without breaking a sweat. There are people who will achieve high scores with relative ease. Most people have to try a little harder. There might not be time to become a maths genius before your assessment centre. However, a few hours of effective preparation can make all the difference between a 'Congratulations!' and a 'Sorry to inform you ...'

Start now, by warming up your numbers brain with some basics.

Skills refresher

There are some basic ways of working with numbers which are the building blocks for all numeracy assessments. This next section will remind you of these skills. Have a go at each example, and then read the explanation.

The four basic rules

Remember learning at a young age how to add, subtract, multiply and divide numbers? Mastering these four arithmetic basics is the foundation of numerical ability. Everything else will follow from this. It is just as easy to work with big numbers as it is with small numbers. The principles are exactly the same.

For most online assessments you will have access to a calculator. *Beware*! It is easy to end up with a decimal point in the wrong place. You still need to have a rough idea of the answer, at least the approximate size of it. For this reason, it is a good idea to polish up your mental maths skills first.

Test your skills 1: Without a calculator

1. Try the following examples, working out the answers without the use of a calculator.
2. Set a timer and see how long this takes you.
3. Then use a calculator to check your answers.

234 + 467 + 975 + 32 = ?	
6943 − 2219 − 630 = ?	
1200 ÷ 20 = ?	
19 × 11 = ?	
963 + ? = 1256	

How did you find this? You will already know the answers from using your calculator. You can find the correct answers and suggestions for dealing with these mental calculations on the next page.

Test your skills 1: Answers

234 + 467 + 975 + 32 = 1708
You might be able to do this in your head by simply adding on each number (and maybe writing down each answer before you add the next, so you don't forget). Or you might use the column method of adding:

```
  234
+ 467
+ 975
+  32
 1708
```

6943 − 2219 − 630 = 4094
As above, you might be able to take away the numbers in your head or prefer the column method:

```
  6943
−2219
  4724
−  630
  4094
```

Or you might find it easier to add together the 2219 and 630 first (as you are going to be taking them both away).
2219 + 630 = 2849

Then 6943 − 2849 = 4094

You might make a rough calculation by rounding up and down:
7000 − 2200 − 630 = 4170
This is useful for questions with multiple choice answers. Just select the one that is closest to your answer.

Or an estimate:
7000 *'ish'* minus 3000 *'ish'* = 4000 *'ish'*

1200 ÷ 20 = 60
In your head you might be able to quickly work out how many 20's you would get in 1200. For some people it helps to picture a practical context, for example, how many £20 notes would there be in a pile totalling £1200.

Or . . . you can start by knocking a '0' off both as 1200 ÷ 20 is the same as 120 ÷ 2.

Or you might easily work out how many times 20 goes into 1000 (50) then add on how many times 20 goes into 200 (10) = 60.

19 × 11 = 209

You can break this down into two sums:
10 × 19 Just add a '0' to times by 10
Plus 1 × 19 (1 times a number is just the number itself)
Estimating – if an estimated answer will do (as it often will in a multiple choice), then you might notice that 19 × 11 can't be that far off 20 × 10 (200).

963 + ? = 1256

This is a little more tricky as the '?' is in a different place. You need to change things around to find out the answer. Make it a subtraction sum instead.
1256 − 963 = 293

How are you feeling at this point? Notice your thoughts and any physical sensations you might be experiencing. A useful state of mind would be positive and determined. Helpful feelings would be a slightly raised level of adrenalin to help you rise to the mental challenge of the timed task.

Numerical assessments (and the questions within) can take a variety of forms. It is a good idea to make yourself familiar with a wide range of different types of assessments. When you are faced with one, you will be able to recognise generally what is expected of you. This will give you a confidence boost.

Some assessments may just ask you to calculate the answers to lots of sums accurately and quickly. You have already tried some basic sums; now look at this trickier example:

Test your skills 2: With a calculator

1. Try the following example: Find the value of '?'.
2. Set a timer and see how long this takes you.
3. Double-check your answer with a calculator (untimed).

$96 \times 8 \div ? + 52 = 68$	_____

How long did it take you to do this? As a guide, the Saville & Holdsworth (SHL a leading test publisher) calculations practice test gives just 18 seconds per question!

You might have noticed that you can't simply punch this sum into your calculator. In order to find out what the question mark stands for, you need to move things around. You might remember that another word for a sum is 'equation', as both sides of the equals sign should be equal in value. This might give you a clue as to how to solve these puzzles. See the table overleaf for an explanation.

Solving equations: Worked examples

Solving equations like this always involves isolating the unknown (?) to one side of the equation, with all the other terms on the other side of the equation.

This involves 'moving' the other terms from one side to the other, which is achieved by using INVERSE operations.

The inverse of + is − ; the inverse of − is +.
The inverse of × is ÷; the inverse of ÷ is ×.

First try it with any small numbers to see what's going on . . .

Example 1: ? + 15 = 20

To isolate '?' you need to move '+ 15' on the left, so carry out the inverse which is '− 15' from *both* sides.
So ? = 5

Example 2: ? × 20 − 5 = 115

(i) Move the '− 5' by using its inverse '+ 5'.
 ? × 20 = 120
(ii) Move '× 20' by using its inverse '÷ 20' on both sides.
 So ? = 6

It's easy when you know how. Now find some more practice examples (see websites at the end of the chapter) and practise doing this quickly.

Test your skills 2: Answer

(96 × 8) ÷ ? + 52 = 68

Multiply numbers in brackets: *768 ÷ ? + 52 = 68*

− 52 both sides: 768 ÷ ? + 52 − 52 = 68 − 52
 768 ÷? = 16
× both sides by '?': 768 ÷ ? × ? = 16 × ?
÷ both sides by 16: 768 ÷ 16 = ?
So, 48 = ?
Or ? = 48

There is often more than one way to solve an equation like the example above. Here are some useful strategies:

- Use common sense: if '?' − 1 =2, then '?' = 2 + 1.
- Do things in a logical order: (2 × 3) + 1 is not the same as 2 × (3 + 1).
- Get to know your calculator and what it can do for you.
- Do the same thing to each side of the equation to keep it balanced, like a see-saw.

As well as helping you with specific calculation questions, brushing up on your calculation skills will help you with more detailed questions.

Some assessments may give you a sequence of numbers, and you need to say what comes next.

In this kind of exercise there are some common sequences using the four basic rules of adding, subtracting, multiplying and dividing. They are a good place to start. Other numbers may be squared (number × number), cubed (number × number × number) or multiplied by itself more times. Prime numbers are worth recognising, as they sometimes crop up. More complex sequences may involve you doing more than one task (for example, double the number and then take away 5). Try these examples.

Numerical sequences: Examples

Look at the following examples. Can you work out the next two numbers in the sequences?

| 20, 40, 80, 160, ?, ? |

| 1, 1, 2, 4, 3, 9, ?, ? |

| 0, 1, 1, 2, 3, 5, 8, 13, ?, ? |

| 2, 3, 5, 7, 11, 13, 17, 19, ?, ? |

The best way to tackle these sequences is to be aware of some of the most common ones, such as the examples above. Beyond that, notice how much bigger (or smaller) the numbers are compared with each other. If they are many times bigger, then you probably need to multiply/

divide. Just try doing something to the number that will get you near to the next number. Then you can adjust it (or if you have a multiple choice of answers, you might be close enough to pick the right one).

Numerical sequences: Answers

20, 40, 80, 160, **320, 640**
Each new number is **double** the previous one.

1, 1, 2, 4, 3, 9, **4, 16**
Ascending numbers are followed by their **square** (the number multiplied by itself).

0, 1, 1, 2, 3, 5, 8, **13, 21, 34**
Each new number equals the two previous numbers added together. This is known as the 'Fibonacci sequence' and is easy to recognise.

2, 3, 5, 7, 11, 13, 17, 19, **23, 29**
These are the 'prime numbers'. Each can only be divided by itself or '1'.

Fractions, decimals and percentages

Many questions will require you to work with fractions, decimals, ratios and percentages. These are all just different measures of proportion. If you can't remember anything at all about proportions, then you might want to start at the very beginning. The BBC Skillswise[3] website has a very helpful section. Understanding proportions is important for lots of problem-solving questions.

The next few pages will help you to revise, or learn, some of the ways in which proportions can be measured. You will see some worked examples. Have a go at each one, even though you can see the answer. This will help you build your confidence. You will also practise swapping between different ways of expressing proportions.

Fractions One way of measuring proportions is fractions. You use fractions every day, for example in sharing things between a number of people or telling the time. You might be required to simplify fractions, especially if you are going to apply the four basic rules $(+ - \times \div)$.

Adding or subtracting fractions: Worked examples

1. Find the **common denominator**.
2. Add or subtract.
3. Reduce (simplify) if necessary.

Example:

A survey shows that $\frac{2}{5}$ of the participants prefer reading, $\frac{1}{4}$ prefer TV and $\frac{1}{3}$ prefer radio.

The remaining participants expressed no preference.
What fraction of participants expressed no preference?
(Reminder: The fractional parts of a whole add up to 1.)

So, $\frac{2}{5} + \frac{1}{4} + \frac{1}{3} + \text{remainder} = 1$

Therefore, $\frac{24}{60} + \frac{15}{60} + \frac{20}{60} + \text{remainder} = 1$

$$\frac{59}{60} + \text{remainder} = 1$$

$$\text{remainder} = 1 - \frac{59}{60} = \frac{1}{60}$$

The fraction of participants expressing 'no preference' is $\frac{1}{60}$.

If 72 preferred to read, how many people took part in the survey?

$$\frac{2}{5} \text{ of total} = 72 \text{ readers}$$

Therefore, total $= 72 \times \frac{5}{2} = 180$

Multiplying or dividing fractions: Worked examples

To multiply: $\quad \frac{a}{b} \times \frac{c}{d} = \frac{a \times c}{b \times d}$

To divide: $\quad \frac{a}{b} \div \frac{c}{d} = \frac{a \times d}{b \times c}$ (invert the divider and change to multiply)

$$= \frac{a \times d}{b \times c}$$

Example:

Jack's rent is £720 per month, which is $\frac{5}{8}$ of his total monthly expenditure (excluding food, clothes and leisure).

His total expenditure (excluding food, clothes and leisure) is $\frac{4}{5}$ of his total income.

a) Express his rent as a fraction of his income
b) Calculate his monthly expenditure (excluding food, clothes and leisure)
c) Calculate his monthly income

Answers:

(a) Rent $= \frac{5}{8}$ of $\frac{4}{5} = \frac{5 \times 4}{8 \times 5} = \frac{1}{2}$ **income**

(b) $\frac{5}{8}$ of expenditure (rent) $= £720$

Therefore, monthly expenditure $= £720 \times \frac{8}{5} = $ **£1152**

(c) $\frac{4}{5}$ of income is monthly expenditure

Therefore, $\frac{4}{5}$ of income $= £1152$

Income $= £1152 \times \frac{5}{4} = $ **£1440**

Chapter 4

Test your skills 3: Solving problems using fractions

Alan, Bess, Charlie and Davina decide to contribute to the shared living costs in proportion to their relative incomes. The total outgoings last month were £2800. Use the information below to calculate how much each pays.

	Alan	Bess	Charlie	Davina
Income (£)	900	1200	1500	2000

(a)	Alan	_____
(b)	Bess	_____
(c)	Charlie	_____
(d)	Davina	_____

Once you have tried this example, check your answers later in the chapter.

Decimals You already use decimals every day, for example using money or metric measurements. You may be required to change a decimal into a fraction or a fraction into a decimal in order to answer some questions. See if you can follow the examples presented here.

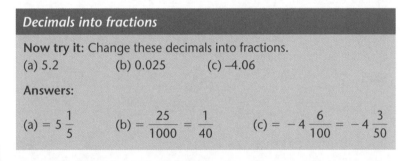

Decimals into fractions

Now try it: Change these decimals into fractions.
(a) 5.2   (b) 0.025   (c) –4.06

Answers:

$$(a) = 5\frac{1}{5} \qquad (b) = \frac{25}{1000} = \frac{1}{40} \qquad (c) = -4\frac{6}{100} = -4\frac{3}{50}$$

Reminder:

To **change a decimal into a fraction**, count the number of places following the decimal point.

If **one** place, then the fraction will be **tenths.**

If **two** places, the fraction will be **hundredths.**

If **three** places, the fraction will be **thousandths**, and so on.

You have just practised changing decimals into fractions. To reverse this and change a fraction into a decimal, you need to divide the numerator (top number) by the denominator (bottom number). You can quickly do this on a calculator, if not in your head. A common mistake is to get the number of decimal places wrong, so try to estimate the scale of the answer you should end up with.

So how are you finding this? It may be that you are reactivating your primary school brain. Decimals and fractions are the basics of numeracy. Reminding yourself of the basic principles in this way will get your brain in gear for numerical tests. If it seems too basic, then remember these are just the building blocks for numeracy. If you are thinking that decimals and fractions are fiendish, keep going. They can transform from fiend to friend with familiarity.

If you are really stuck, then you might need more in-depth help to figure it out. See the suggestions at the end of the chapter.

> ### Reminder:
>
> Revising your times tables will really save you time in many different kinds of sums.

Percentages You will be very familiar with percentages as your academic achievement will frequently have been measured and expressed in this form of numbers. Percentages are basically fractions in which the denominator is always 100 and is written as %.

Here are some examples:

$$\frac{25}{100} = 25\%$$

$$3\frac{3}{10} = 3\frac{30}{100} = 330\%$$

$$0.23 = \frac{23}{100} = 23\%$$

$$0.025 = \frac{2.5}{100} = 2.5\%$$

> ### Reminder:
>
> To change a decimal into a percentage: multiply by 100.
>
> To change a fraction into a percentage: first change it into a decimal, then multiply by 100.
>
> To change a percentage into a decimal: divide by 100.

Look at the following examples to practise this skill.

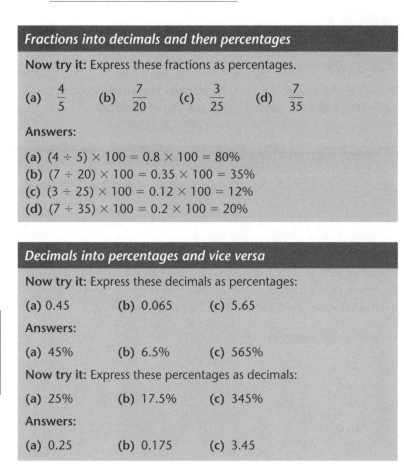

Fractions into decimals and then percentages

Now try it: Express these fractions as percentages.

(a) $\dfrac{4}{5}$ (b) $\dfrac{7}{20}$ (c) $\dfrac{3}{25}$ (d) $\dfrac{7}{35}$

Answers:

(a) $(4 \div 5) \times 100 = 0.8 \times 100 = 80\%$
(b) $(7 \div 20) \times 100 = 0.35 \times 100 = 35\%$
(c) $(3 \div 25) \times 100 = 0.12 \times 100 = 12\%$
(d) $(7 \div 35) \times 100 = 0.2 \times 100 = 20\%$

Decimals into percentages and vice versa

Now try it: Express these decimals as percentages:

(a) 0.45   (b) 0.065   (c) 5.65

Answers:

(a) 45%   (b) 6.5%   (c) 565%

Now try it: Express these percentages as decimals:

(a) 25%   (b) 17.5%   (c) 345%

Answers:

(a) 0.25   (b) 0.175   (c) 3.45

Now test out what you have learned.

Test your skills 4: Percentages

Change these decimals into percentages.	
(a) 0.35	(a) _____
(b) 0.025	(b) _____
(c) 12.50	(c) _____

So that's a refresher on percentages. Practise using your calculator to make quick calculations of percentages so that it becomes second nature.

Hopefully, it is starting to make sense. Check the answers to 'Test Your Skills 3 and 4'.

Test your skills 3: Answers

Combined earnings = £5 600

Individual incomes as fractions of combined income:

Alan $= \dfrac{900}{5600}$ Bess $= \dfrac{1200}{5600}$ Charlie $= \dfrac{1500}{5600}$

Davina $= \dfrac{2000}{5600}$

Individual costs:

Alan = £2800 $\times \dfrac{900}{5600}$ = £450; Bess = £2800 $\times \dfrac{1200}{5600}$ = £600

Charlie £2800 $\times = \dfrac{1500}{5600}$ = £750

Davina = £2800 $\times \dfrac{2000}{5600}$ = £1000

(Alternatively, because total outgoings form half of the total income, then everyone contributes half their income.)

Test your skills 4: Answers

(a) $0.35 \times 100 = 35\%$
(b) $0.025 \times 100 = 2.5\%$
(c) $12.50 \times 100 = 1250\%$

To calculate 5% of a sum: Calculate 10%, and then halve it.

To calculate 1% of a sum: Calculate 10%, and then divide by 10.

Most other percentages can easily be worked out from manipulating the above.

For example:

$17\% = 10\% + 5\% + 2 \times 1\%$

Useful strategy: To calculate 10% of a sum

If there is a decimal point, move it one place to the left, or if there is no decimal point, place one before the final digit.

Examples:

10% of 31.5   = 3.15

10% of 3.60   = 0.36

10% of 65   = 6.5

10% of 324   = 32.4

Percentage calculations often appear as 'profit and loss'–type questions. It is important, when faced with this type of question, that you read carefully what is being asked of you. You may be given an 'original measure' (e.g. in £s) and then asked to increase or decrease it by a given percentage to find a new amount. Alternatively, you may be asked to calculate the percentage by which a new figure has increased or decreased in relation to the original measure. Remembering how to work these types of questions out quickly will help save you time and stress.

Percentage addition (includes growth, increase, profit, interest, etc.)

A measure in its original state is thought of as being 100%.

If you increase it by 10%, for example, it is now 100% + 10%. The increased amount is 110% of the original amount.

$$100\% + 10\% = 110\% \times \text{Original}$$
$$= \frac{110}{100} \times \text{Original}$$
$$= 1.10 \times \text{Original}$$

Percentage subtraction (shrinkage, decrease, loss, etc.)

A measure that is reduced by 25%, for example, is now 100% − 25% of the original amount; that is, 75% of the original amount.

$$100\% - 25\% = 75\% \times \text{Original}$$
$$= \frac{75}{100} \times \text{Original}$$
$$= 0.75 \times \text{Original}$$

Expressing an amount as a percentage of some greater amount (profit, loss)

% increase = (actual increase ÷ original amount) × 100

% decrease = (actual decrease ÷ original amount) × 100

Take a look at the examples that follow.

Example 1:

An item in an online auction increases from £34 to £52.50. Work out the percentage **increase** to the nearest percentage point:

Actual increase (£52.50 – £34) = £18.50

Percentage increase   = £18.50 ÷ £34 × 100

                            = 54% increase

Example 2:

A coat is reduced from £42 to £18. Work out the percentage **reduction** to the nearest point.

Actual decrease (£42 − £18)   = £24

Percentage reduction   = £24 ÷ £42 × 100

                       = 57.14% reduction

Rounded to the nearest % = 57%

Remember to round up if the decimal is 0.5 or above, and round down if it is below 0.5.

Remember that for quick estimates of calculations, it's useful to round up or down. For example, £42 reduced to £18 is almost £40 to £20, which is 50%. This is often sufficient for multiple choice answers.

Test your skills 5: % increase and decrease

Now try these:

(a) Over a period of 1 month, a flower increases its mass by 25%. At the beginning of the month, it weighed 130 g. What did it weigh after 1 month?

(b) Over a period of 6 months, a dieter loses 5% of his weight. At the beginning of his diet, he weighed 90 kg. What is his weight after 6 months?

Chapter 4

Test your skills 5: Answers

(a) $130 \times 1.25 = 162.5$ g
(b) $90 \times 0.95 = 85.5$ kg

Next, take a look at ratios.

Ratios A ratio expresses a fixed relationship between two or more measures. Ratios can be treated like fractions. They have equivalents and may be reduced to simpler forms. They may also be expressed as a fraction.

The simplest ratios involve two measures, for example (4:5). Other ratios can involve more than two measures, for example (3:5:6:11…).

Here's an example: Twenty-four-carat gold is a mixture of pure gold to other metals in the ratio 3:1. Three parts pure gold is mixed with 1 part of another metal or metals. This means that 24-carat gold is 75% pure gold. Three parts in every four are pure gold. So, the ratio of pure gold to the rest is, $\frac{3}{4} : \frac{1}{4}$ or simply 3:1.

Similarly, using ratios you can work out proportional quantities. Take a look at the next example.

Ratios to find related quantities: An example

The ratio of men to women in a choir is 2:5.
Clearly, there are more women than men. In fact:

The number of women   = Number of men $\times \dfrac{5}{2}$

The number of men   = Number of women $\times \dfrac{2}{5}$

If the number of women is 25, how many men are in this choir?

The number of men   = Number of women $\times \dfrac{2}{5}$

$= 25 \times \dfrac{2}{5} = 10$

If the number of men is 20, how many women are in this choir?

The number of women   = Number of men $\times \dfrac{5}{2}$

$= 20 \times \dfrac{5}{2} = 50$

One practical application of decimals and ratios is currency conversion. To convert between currencies, simply multiply by the exchange rate.

Converting currency: An example

Convert £100 into euros at an exchange rate of £1 to €1.36.

£100 × 1.36 = €136

Convert €75 into pounds at an exchange rate of €1 to £0.74.

€75 × 0.74 = £55.50

Now test yourself on the next example.

Test your skills 6: Ratios

Try this:

The ratio of miles to kilometres is approximately 5:8.

(a) Approximately how many kilometres are equivalent to 26 miles?

(b) Approximately how many miles are equivalent to 72 kilometres?

Kilometres = Miles × $\dfrac{8}{5}$

Miles = Kilometres × $\dfrac{5}{8}$

Reminder: When ratios have more than two measures, the total number of 'parts' in the situation must be considered.

Example 1: The ratio of 2:5 has a total of 7 parts (2 + 5).

Example 2: The ratio 5:7:8 has a total of 20 parts.

Ratio: Divide into parts

Try this:
Divide £150 in the ratio 7:5:3.

Answer:
Value of one part = £150 ÷ (7 + 5 + 3)

= £10

The amounts   = £70, £50 and £30

It's a common mistake to confuse a ratio with a fraction. So, for example, in the question on page 74 where the ratio of men to women is 2:5, the fraction of the choir that is men is $\frac{2}{7}$ and **not** $\frac{2}{5}$.

Test your skills 6: Answers

(a) 26 miles in kilometres $= 26 \times \dfrac{8}{5} = 41.6$ kilometres

(b) 72 kilometres in miles $= 72 \times \dfrac{5}{8} = 45$ miles

---

You may be thinking that this is all just basic arithmetic but numerical tests take these skills further when they require you to apply numerical principles to scenarios or problems.

Now you've covered some of the basics and you might feel that you need to take a break. You've started your training. Are you ready to take it to the next level?

Taking it to the next level

Now that you can recognise basic things you can do with numbers, you will be able to tackle most assessments. There are different types of numerical ability questions, but there are often similar patterns. They all use the basic building blocks of numeracy. By trying lots of different examples you will be able to quickly spot what you need to do.

Problem-solving with numbers Some questions will place the numbers in a practical context. You will have to spot the relevant information and decide what to do with it. Often the question will be business or finance related. It may involve using what you know about proportions to calculate interest rates or profit and loss. Don't worry if you know nothing at all about the particular industry. You won't be expected to. But do you know the difference between *simple* and *compound* interest? If you don't, then be careful if you are thinking of borrowing money!

Consider simple interest calculations first. Look at the example.

Simple interest: The basics

Simple interest is when a sum multiplied by an interest rate multiplied by a number of time units.
For example £P at I % interest over N years. Where
P = the principal (or original) sum
I = the percentage interest rate
N = the number of time units (years, months and so on)
Then, total interest accrued = **P × I × N**

Simple interest: An example

£10,000 is invested and accrues **simple** interest at the rate of 5% per annum. Calculate the value of the investment after 6 years?

P = £10,000   I = 5% N = 6 years

Total interest accrued   = P × I × N

$$= £10,000 \times \frac{5}{100} \times 6$$

$$= £10,000 \times 0.05 \times 6$$

$$= £3,000$$

Value of the investment   = £10,000 + interest accrued

$$= £10,000 + £3,000$$

$$= £13,000$$

Compound interest involves a cumulative effect, so the bigger the sum gets, the more interest is added. Interest is added to the original (principal) amount, so then the added interest also accrues interest at the end of each accounting period (such as the year). This increased amount is the new principal for the following accounting period.

Chapter 4

Compound interest: An example

£8,000 is invested for 3 years at **compound** interest rate of 5%. Calculate the value of the investment after 3 years:

$$P = £8,000$$
$$I = 5\% \, (0.05)$$
$$N = 3 \text{ years}$$

Year 1: Principal = £8,000
Interest gained = £8,000 × 0.05 = £400

Year 2: Principal = £8,400
Interest gained = £8,400 × 0.05 = £420

Year 3: Principal = £8,820
Interest gained = £8,820 × 0.05 = £441

Total interest accrued = £1,261
Value of investment = £9,261

Now that you understand this cumulative effect, it can also apply to other practical applications. For example, if the flower in 'Test your skills 5' gained mass cumulatively (i.e. multiplying by 25% each month), it would be growing more quickly than if it gained 25% of the original weight each month.

Start: 130g
End of month 1: 130g + 25% = 162.5g
End of month 2: 162.5g + 25% = 203.125g and so on

Making sense of charts and tables Data-interpretation-type tests often show you information which may be in the form of numbers or in a table, graph or chart. A common type of question will give you data in a business context, and you need to manipulate numbers, often using different skills, to find the correct answer. For example, they may tell you how many items a factory makes in a year, the factory costs and annual profits. A starter question may be just to work out the profit per item (simple division). A more advanced question could ask you to consider the impact of some kind of change in circumstances (e.g. an increase in production costs, a fall in sales or something similar). You will need to use more complex calculations to work out new figures. A common mistake is not to read the question fully and to spend valuable time doing unnecessary calculations.

Next, it's useful to practise at profit and loss calculations, a common test question for commercial careers.

Working out profit: An example

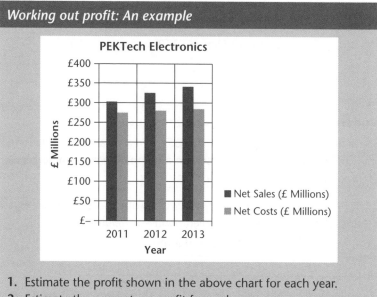

1. Estimate the profit shown in the above chart for each year.
2. Estimate the percentage profit for each year.

Working out profits In simple terms, profit is worked out as the total income minus any associated costs.

Profit = total income (£) − total costs (£)

To determine the percentage profit, you would take the amount of profit and divide that by actual sales then multiply by 100.

Percentage profit = profit (£) ÷ sales (£) × 100

Working out profit: Answers

(1) Profit: 2011 = £300m − £275m = £25m

2012 = £325m − £280m = £45m

2013 = £340m − £285m = £55m

Use these answers below to work out the % profit.

(2) % Profit: 2011 = £25m ÷ £300m × 100 = 8.33%

2012 = £45m ÷ £325m × 100 = 13.85%

2013 = £55m ÷ £340m × 100 = 16.18%

Understanding trends and relationships

Some questions may ask you to interpret *trends* by studying relationships between measures expressed on a graph. There are three common results of this type of analysis:

1. The measures are *directly proportional*. As one measure increases, so does the other. This is also called *positive correlation*.

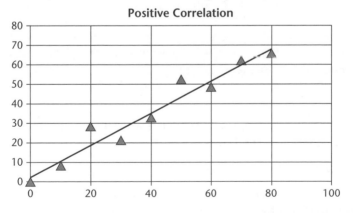

2. The measures are *inversely proportional*. As one measure increases, the other decreases. This is called *negative correlation*.

Negative Correlation

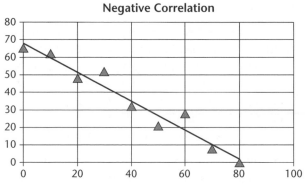

3. The measures *do not correlate*: they appear to be distributed randomly. There does not seem to be a relationship between the two, so if one increases it shouldn't affect the other at all.

No Correlation

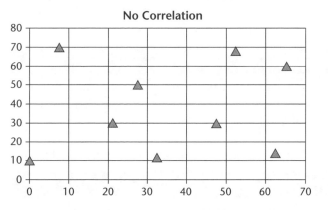

Take a look at the chart below. Make an initial analysis of what could be assumed.

Ice cream sales: Your analysis

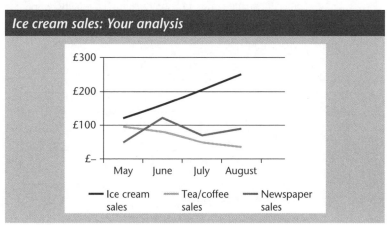

So what can be assumed from this chart?

In the above chart, the sales of ice cream positively correlate with the progression of months during summer. As summer proceeds, the sales of ice cream increase. Conversely, as the summer progresses, the sale of hot drinks falls. This is a negative correlation. Sales of newspapers seem not to correlate. It is tempting to interpret the changing sales of ice cream and hot drinks as caused by rising temperatures. However, correlation does not necessarily prove causality. That is a more complex task.

Interpreting relationships – a warning One possible explanation for the sales increase is that consumers associate ice cream with summer and holidays. Or perhaps ice cream advertisements are more prevalent during the summer months? Or a new brand was launched? Or electricity prices dropped and so did the price of ice cream? In other words, you need to base assumptions of relationships on the facts given, *not* your own experience or expectations.

Negative marking

Some tests may deduct points for incorrect answers, which makes guessing a risky strategy. These sorts of tests are quite unusual, but if in doubt, ask the test provider.

Now test your skills in interpreting information presented in tables.

Test your skills 7: Table interpretation

Consider the accident data below.

Accident Data			
	Casualty count	Casualty count	Casualty count
Year	Thistown	Thattown	Tothertown
Population*	60000	36000	80000
2013	90	36	75
2012	95	41	91
2011	101	46	99
2010	119	51	110
2009	120	60	125
Total (2009–2013)	525	234	500

*Assume stability of populations over the time period

You will often find items like this that begin with fairly easy questions, building up to more complex, multi-step calculations. The trick is to make the most of it and score the easy points. Also, read the questions carefully so that you don't waste time making calculations that are unnecessary. The final question is not numerical, but asks you to think logically. This will help you to prepare for the next chapter on verbal reasoning.

Test your skills 7: Table interpretation questions

1. How many casualties occurred in Thattown during 2011?

2. In which year were overall casualties of all three towns 246?

3. For each town, estimate the percentage change in casualties per thousand from 2009 to 2013.

4. Which town showed the lowest percentage reduction in casualties per thousand of the population from 2009 to 2013?

5. Suggest any other information you may need to determine which town performed the least well in road safety overall.

Chapter 4

So how did you do with this skills test?

Test your skills 7: Answers

(1) 46 casualties

(2) Year 2011

	Population	Casualties/1000		Actual change/1000
	How many thousands	2009 A	2013 B	(A – B)
Thistown	60	$\dfrac{120}{60}$	$\dfrac{90}{60}$	$\dfrac{120}{60} - \dfrac{90}{60} = \dfrac{1}{2}$
Thattown	36	$\dfrac{60}{36}$	$\dfrac{36}{36}$	$\dfrac{60}{36} - \dfrac{36}{36} = \dfrac{2}{3}$
Tothertown	80	$\dfrac{125}{80}$	$\dfrac{75}{80}$	$\dfrac{125}{80} - \dfrac{75}{80} = \dfrac{5}{8}$

(3) % change = actual change ÷ original measure × 100

% change Thistown $= \dfrac{1}{2} \div \dfrac{120}{60} \times 100 = 25\%$

% change Thattown $= \dfrac{2}{3} \div \dfrac{60}{36} \times 100 = 40\%$

% change Tothertown $= \dfrac{5}{8} \div \dfrac{125}{80} \times 100 = 40\%$

(4) Lowest percentage change is Thistown at 25%

(5) Any reasonable answer: industrial versus rural town; age profile of population; quality of infrastructure for example

It may be that you discovered some shortcuts to gaining the correct answer. For example, in Question 2 it is necessary only to sum the last digit of each measure for each year. The answer ending in a '6' must be the correct one. You might have simply estimated the percentage changes by rounding figures up or down. Notice also how you have to use some of those basic arithmetical functions to make sense of the chart questions.

So you now know the basic skills and functions used in numerical tests. Take some time to review the examples and redo the Skills Tests, timing yourself. Review the sections that you found the least easy. You really can learn from your mistakes and find your own ways to deal with these test challenges.

Winning ways

Successful and less successful test candidates recommend certain best strategies for performing well in tests. Here are some ideas.

Create the most conducive environment You may be asked to complete the assessment online to ascertain whether you will be invited to the assessment centre. If this is the case, make sure the time and place is suitable. Do it somewhere with a good Internet connection. Manage potential distractions, including phone calls and messages (it might be better not to use your phone as a calculator). Have a pen and paper handy for jotting down parts of the answers in multi-step sums.

Read the instructions carefully Usually the timing does not start until you click a 'Start' button in online tests. Take this opportunity to take a deep breath and focus upon exactly what you are being asked to do.

Balance speed and accuracy Is it better to complete only a few and get them all right or to whizz through and make lots of errors? The correct answer (usually) is to maintain a balance: to work very quickly, but not so quickly that you make mistakes. Some tests may have an overall time and will tell you which item you are on and how long you have left. Other tests will give you a specific amount of time per question and then move you on.

Check the length of time you have, and consider roughly how long this would give you per question (but don't expect to finish them all).

Skim-read the question Assess what exactly it is asking you to do. You don't want to waste time making irrelevant calculations. Many numerical assessments will show a chart or table of data, for example, and you need to work out an answer about one or two of the variables on it (a variable is just something that can vary, such as a cost, a size, a percentage, etc.), but you have to know what to focus on and what to ignore.

Don't panic Some numerical assessments are just sums 'dressed up' in words which will probably be about a context unfamiliar to you (such as manufacturing production, meteorological conditions or marketing). This doesn't matter. In fact, *not* being an expert on this subject can be an advantage, as it allows you to see through the blurb to the numbers.

Make your best guess and move on You may find some questions are easier than others (they may become progressively harder or may be presented randomly). If you read a question and have absolutely no idea how to even begin to tackle it, then don't waste valuable time. Make your best guess before time runs out. Some tests may allow you to go back to previous items; others won't. Be smart.

Reflection

To maximise your learning, it's useful to reflect upon your performance and identify where you need to improve. Think about how you can improve your performance, based on what you have discovered through an honest review. There are some useful questions you could ask yourself. Work through the questions and record your answers. This will help you reflect in a structured way.

Chapter 4

Test review: Improve your performance

1. How did it go overall? What did I do well?

2. How was I feeling before, during and after the test? Did this hinder my performance?

3. What was I saying to myself? (It's normal – but unhelpful – to listen to your critical inner voice.)

4. Were there any questions that I had no idea how to tackle? What were they? How can I learn how to do them?

5. Did I manage my time well? What could I do to improve this?

6. As a result of this review, what can I do to improve my performance next time?

Now, taking into account your review, take an honest look at the skills below, and consider which are your strengths, average abilities (okay) and weaknesses (tick the box):

Skill	Weakness	Okay	Strength
Staying calm and positive			
Balancing speed and accuracy			
Basic arithmetic ($+ - \div \times$)			
Using a calculator for trickier sums			
Number sequences			
Proportions (fractions, %, decimals and ratios)			
Applied proportions (interest rates, profits)			
Reading and understanding graphs, charts and tables			
Reflecting and learning something positive from experiences			

Best strategies

Does practice make perfect? Not necessarily! Just doing things wrong over and over again won't help you to get it right. You need to know where you went wrong and how to do it right, which is where some practice tests fall down and can actually lower your confidence (which isn't helpful).

Choose websites and books which help you to develop skills They will tell/show you the answers, as you have experienced here. Then progress to the timed practice tests which employers and test publishers provide.

Remember You may not be competing with other people sitting next to you, but against a normative score based upon thousands of people who have already done the test. Everyone around you might get through ... or nobody! You probably won't know how many you need to get right in order to pass, and this will depend upon a number of things such as:

- The job you are being recruited for
- The level of numeracy required
- The number of vacancies in that role
- The general level of competition for that recruitment phase
- How the company use the tests. For some it is a strict pass or fail. Others will consider the results as just one piece of information to be taken into account along with degree class and quality of the application form.

The assessment may be checking for an ability level which is at least 'average' rather than super-genius!

Get some perspective Just because you don't get through a graduate-level numerical ability assessment does not mean you are no good at maths. Try a range of assessments of different abilities at various levels to get some sense of perspective. Some of these tests are pitched at a very high level simply because graduate jobs are highly competitive. Selectors need to find ways to identify the difference between people. These tests are an incomplete or partial representation of your intelligence. They are not a reflection upon your value as a person, your potential for success as a graduate or anything other than the very specific thing they are designed to measure.

Time for a rethink? If you really dislike working with numbers, and the jobs you are going for keep requiring high-level numerical skills, then maybe it is time for a rethink. Numeracy is just one skill. You have many others. What are you really good at and what do you most enjoy doing? Many highly successful people accept that numbers aren't their favourite things and they simply choose careers which play to their strengths.

Remember too that graduate schemes represent only a small, although very prominent and visible, portion of the opportunities available to you. They are not the be-all and end-all. Many small and medium-sized enterprises (SMEs) don't use these tests (usually because they are very expensive). Also jobs with SMEs are not as widely advertised, so you may face less competition. Working in a smaller company can have many advantages. For example, promotion prospects and job satisfaction can be better.

It's not the end of the world if you don't pass the assessments. Honestly. Many highly successful people failed tests. In fact, sometimes that failure made them even more determined.

Numerical ability assessments are all about testing your number skills. You will have noticed that they contain words too. This means you also need to be able to understand sentences and pick out the facts to solve the problem. The next chapter will help you to brush up on your verbal reasoning skills.

Employer's view – graduate recruiter for a leading supermarket

We select candidates with a versatile skill profile so we can place them anywhere within in the organisation, now and in the future.

My advice to candidates is not to underestimate the level and the time pressure of ability assessments. If you haven't done any timed tests for a while, don't expect to sit down and fly through it. Go online, find practice tests and spend a couple of hours preparing in order to give yourself the best chance of success.

Be commercially savvy. Understand concepts such as profit and loss. Do your research on the company, its 5-year plan and where it sits within the market. You could have a great degree, do well on the assessments then fall down in the interview.

Be able to adapt your thinking. Some numerical assessments use 'dollars' rather than 'pounds' in questions. The process is exactly the same.

Ability assessments are usually the first hurdle. If you fall, pick yourself up and learn from it. You can always apply again next year.

Chapter 4

Summary of best advice

Psych yourself up: Put aside any doubts about your numerical ability. Think of this as an obstacle course where stamina and determination are just as important as skills. And the prize could be the job of your dreams!

Do some maths every day: Add up and estimate the shopping bill as you put it in your basket. Watch numerical quiz shows. Do number puzzles. Say times tables out loud. Look at a bill, bank statement or pay slip, and check you understand where all the numbers come from.

Discover the joy of numbers: There is a great satisfaction in arriving at a tangible answer. Seeing it listed in the multi-choice answers of a test is very reassuring.

Get some books or online guides: First, look at ones which show you how, before you take practice tests.

Get lots of practice: Every job you apply for (and don't get) is practice.

Read instructions carefully: And read the question fully so you don't waste time doing calculations you don't need.

Make good use of your time: If you have no idea how to even begin to tackle a question, make your best guess and move on.

Balance speed and accuracy: You won't have time to work everything out fully. Shortcuts and estimations will help.

Reflect your performance: After every practice (or real) assessment, make a point of learning more about the things you got stuck on.

Keep a sense of perspective: It really isn't the end of the world if you just don't get it.

Get professional help: Seek out the right support in understanding numbers, building your confidence or getting into a job that's right for you.

Find out more

- **Kent University Careers Service**
  http://www.kent.ac.uk/careers/tests/mathstest.htm
  There are really good examples and explanations of numerical

ability tests on this website, as well as some which combine verbal and numerical abilities (verbal logic and logical reasoning).

- **BBC Skillswise**
  http://www.bbc.co.uk/skillswise/maths
  This is a great website aimed at adults who want to improve everyday numerical skills. You may find the proportions section useful if you need to know more about the basics of fractions.

- **Mathcentre**
  http://www.mathcentre.ac.uk
  This is a really useful website set up by universities to help people in post-16 education to refresh and update their mathematical skills. There are multi-media resources (including a downloadable numeracy refresher booklet), and it is all free.

- **SHL Direct – practice tests**
  www.shldirect.com/en/practice-tests
  Saville and Holdsworth Talent Measurement is one of the most widely used psychometric test providers and publishes a range of practice tests online. The quick calculations test is very interesting to try.

- **Assessment Day**
  www.assessmentday.co.uk
  A brilliant website created by two students based upon their experience of preparing for and attending graduate assessment centres. It includes realistic examples of tests written by test developers.

- **Learndirect**
  www.learndirect.com
  If you would like to brush up on your maths skills (particularly if you haven't got GCSE maths), then find a local course on this website.

- **Numerical Reasoning Test**
  http://www.numericalreasoningtest.org/
  Good explanation of the history and science behind numerical assessments. Also offers some realistic practice examples.

Please note: The examples used in this chapter are purely for illustrative purposes. Real psychometric assessments are scientifically constructed and tested to make sure that they are valid for the intended purpose.

Chapter 4

What to do next

If you are still feeling unsure:

Find a maths course or local tutor if you need more individual support and you are willing to invest some time in improving your numerical skills.

Get help from your university study support unit who can help you to overcome numerical and verbal difficulties, especially if you have a learning disability, English is not your first language, or you are a mature student who hasn't studied maths for a long time.

'Buddy up': if you are good at English but weaker in maths, find a friend who is good at Maths and weaker in English, and support each other.

If you are fairly confident but still have room for improvement:

Check out websites and books which offer further practice and skill development (see above).

If you are capable, calm and confident:

Brilliant! Go for it (but don't let complacency stop you from reading things carefully or lead you to make you overly rush through answers).

Verbal reasoning assessments

Contents

It's hard to think of any job which doesn't require the ability to communicate using language. That's why you are very likely to encounter an assessment of your verbal reasoning in an assessment centre.

Verbal reasoning tests can assess your ability to:

- Understand different meanings of words.
- Be clear about principles of grammar.
- Pick out key facts in a piece of text.
- Decide on the inferences contained within a written passage.
- Do all of the above quickly and accurately.

This chapter will help you to identify, develop and practise your verbal reasoning skills. You will notice that you already use these skills every day in your work, study and personal life. This will help you to feel more confident and prepared for these assessments.

In Chapter 3 you looked at some basic examples. Now you can take this to another level by understanding what will be expected of you and learning some useful techniques.

Confidence with words

Acquiring and interpreting language is a skill which comes naturally to you. You probably know around 20 000–35 000 words! You are probably still learning new words every day without even trying. So how can you get even better at understanding words? And, most importantly, how can you perform at your best when under pressure? Take a moment to make a quick guess about your confidence with words. How would you score yourself on a scale of 1–10 for your verbal confidence? Note this rating down. The Skills Refresher section below is a good place to start to build your confidence and improve your rating. It will help you know what skills you will use in a verbal reasoning test.

Skills refresher

Basic verbal tests

Words with the same or opposite meanings   A **synonym** is a word that has the same meaning as another. It's just like a basic crossword clue where you have to think of a word with a similar meaning. For example, the word 'happy' is similar in meaning to the word 'elated'.

An **antonym** is a word that is the opposite in meaning to a particular word. For example, the word 'happy' is the opposite of the word 'melancholy'.

You may be shown one word and then asked to choose from a list of words, deciding which words mean the same (synonym) or which mean the opposite of the original word (antonym).

Try the examples.

Example 1: Synonyms

Reticent

Which of the following words means the **same** as, or is similar to, the word above:

a) Correct
b) Restrained
c) Unreserved
d) Ambivalent

Example 2: Antonyms

Permit

Which of the following words means the **opposite** of the word above:

a) Pass
b) Change
c) Engage
d) Prohibit

So how can you improve your confidence with words and meanings? It's useful to expand your vocabulary by using the Thesaurus feature on your computer. Make a habit of checking words and those that have similar or opposite meanings. Aim to expand your use of words so that you can add variety to anything you write. Of course, this will also help with these kinds of tests.

Spelling, grammar and punctuation You might find you are required to check a passage of text for errors of spelling, grammar and/or punctuation. These can seem obvious, but it is easy to overlook minor errors or common misspellings. Scan and check the next example. How many errors can you pick up?

Example 3: Spelling and grammar

Correct the following passage by adding appropriate spelling, punctuation and grammar:

You might think that spelling and gramma aren't important in applying for job's. Well you wood be wrong. many employer's selection proceses include an preliminiary sift. There time is to valuable to waste on people who cant be bothered too proofread what theyve writen that's why i always defiantly insure that I check evrything throughly

Check your answers now. Notice your strengths and weaknesses. Decide how you can improve.

Chapter 5

Answers: Synonyms and antonyms

Example 1:
'Reticent' is the same as or similar to (b) Restrained

Example 2:
'Permit' is the opposite of (d) Prohibit

Answers: Spelling and grammar

Example 3:

You might think that spelling and grammar aren't important in applying for jobs. Well, you would be wrong. Many employers' selection processes include a preliminary sift. Their time is too valuable to waste on people who can't be bothered to proofread what they've written. That's why I always definitely ensure that I check everything thoroughly.

Common spelling and grammar mistakes

Example 3 shows some mistakes which are very easy to make. They often appear on CVs, believe it or not. If you are applying for a role which requires strong written communication (e.g. in media or sales) you may face this kind of activity. It could be in the form of a test or an in-tray exercise.

Common spelling and grammar mistakes	
Incorrect spelling	Simply spelling a word wrong
Incorrect spelling – similar words	Make sure you know the difference between **homonyms**, words which sound the same but are spelt differently: To/too/two There/their/they're Ensure/insure

Incorrect use of apostrophes (')	An apostrophe can indicate that words have been shortened (e.g. cannot – can't). It can also indicate that something belongs or is linked to something else (e.g. an employer's or many employers' selection process/es)
Lazy use of the spell check function	A word exists, so it is not automatically highlighted as an error. Or a similar but incorrect word is suggested as a substitute (e.g. 'defiantly' instead of 'definitely').

If you feel you need further help with your spelling and grammar, websites such as BBC Skillswise[1] are worth a visit.

Taking it to the next level

Verbal reasoning tests are an extension of basic verbal tests. You will be asked to show your understanding by deciding on the accuracy of statements related to a piece of writing. Each piece of text will be featured in a question. There will be about 30 questions. It will be timed. You may not complete all the questions. Typically you will be allowed 20 minutes for 30 questions. There will be clear instructions, a practice example and an online timer. Check the instructions.

The written text pieces

These will come from a range of sources. The topics may be unfamiliar or even familiar. Try hard to disregard what you already know about that topic. You have to focus on what is contained in that piece of text. Answer the questions based on what you understand to be true or false, as indicated in that piece of writing. What you think is true or false about the topic may mislead you. Decide your conclusion solely based on the details in the written statement.

It's useful to allow a minute per question as a starting point.

Remember the example of ice cream sales from the previous chapter? It is easy to jump to conclusions about how facts relate to each other. Be a 'truth detective'. Look for evidence that would prove a conclusion beyond all reasonable doubt.

The statements

There will usually be five or six statements to consider. You will be required to decide whether the statements are *True, False* or if there is INSUFFICIENT EVIDENCE offered. For example, you will choose between buttons on an online test that show *True, False, Cannot say* or DEFINITELY *True,* UN*True,* INSUFFICIENT INFO or something similar.

Here's a quick example.

Verbal reasoning test 1

Health experts maintain that eating five fruits and vegetables a day is good for you. There needs to be more clarity about what constitutes one portion of fruit or vegetable. It's too confusing for consumers. If oranges are good, why is too much orange juice bad?

Decide if the following statement is *True, False* or *Cannot say* (because there is no evidence either way).

Consumers are confused about oranges.

Reasoning out the statement

On the basis of this text, you might be tempted to select *True* for this statement. This would be a misreading of the text. Sometimes a statement may seem too obvious. In this case, it is impossible to decide if this is *True* or *False* without more information. The best decision answer would be *Cannot say*. The statement given is a speculative claim or opinion. There is actually no evidence that consumers are confused. You may be confused by health guidelines. Don't let this influence your judgement. Now try the next example.

Verbal reasoning test 2

Decide which statements are *True* (T), *False* (F) or *Cannot say* (CS) (because there is no evidence either way).

Prosthetists are part of a rehabilitation team and are involved in assessing a patient to see what will be required to enable the person to manage without a particular limb or body part.

An orbital prosthetist might take measurements and place a special mould or cast in the empty eye socket to ensure that a false eye will fit perfectly. Once the new eye is made, according to specifications taken by the prosthetist, the orbital prosthetist will fit the eye and advise on its care.

Similarly, in fitting a new limb, the prosthetist will talk to the patient and take detailed measurements and shape-sensing tracings, so that the design of the limb can be as perfect as possible. Further adjustments can be made as the patient becomes used to the appliance or false limb/part.

	T, F or CS
Statement 1: Prosthetists only get involved with the fitting of false limbs or body parts.	
Statement 2: Prosthetists need to be sensitive and tactful.	
Statement 3: A prosthetist works to detailed tolerance limits.	
Statement 4: Having to be measured for a false limb is embarrassing and discomforting.	
Statement 5: Adjustments to the prosthesis can be made once a patient has used it for a while.	

So how did you find this test? Notice how you have to think hard about what is actually in the piece of text. You need to focus strictly on what is contained in the passage and what is not. Keep asking yourself the question 'What is the evidence for this statement?'

Check the answers below to see how you did.

Focus on the facts contained in the text you are given.

Keep aside your own knowledge about the topic.

Answers: Verbal reasoning test 2

Statement 1: *False* – They assess patients and help in the whole rehabilitation process.

Statement 2: *Cannot say* – This is a false assumption which is unsubstantiated by the passage.

Statement 3: *True* – There is evidence in the passage 'detailed measurements and shape-sensing traces'.

Statement 4: *Cannot say* – This is a false assumption, which is unsubstantiated by the passage.

Statement 5: *True* – There is evidence in the passage in the final sentence 'Further adjustments …'.

Try the next example, and remember to notice the key words and phrases, which are actual facts contained within the passage. You need to strive to avoid any false assumptions that you may be tempted to make.

Verbal reasoning test 3 (100 words)

Decide which statements are *True* (T), *False* (F) or *Cannot say* (CS).

The perfusionist is a skilled health professional who is trained as a member of the surgical team to set up and operate the heart-lung machinery, including auto-transfusion units that prevent blood loss during operations. When a patient's heart has to be stopped in open-heart surgery, the patient's blood has to be taken out of the body through the heart-lung machine. The perfusionist is responsible for the operation of this machine during surgery and has to monitor circulation, take action if required and communicate with the surgeon and anaesthetist. Equipment used is highly technological and may be mechanical or electronic. Perfusionists literally do hold a patient's life in their hands.

	T, F or CS
Statement 1: A perfusionist deals with life-or-death situations.	
Statement 2: The perfusionist is as qualified as a doctor or anaesthetist.	
Statement 3: The perfusionist is responsible for the auto-transfusion unit.	
Statement 4: The perfusionist monitors the circulation of a patient during an operation.	
Statement 5: The auto-transfusion unit collects blood from the patient during the operation and cleans it of impurities.	

Answers: Verbal reasoning test 3

Statement 1: *True* – This is a reasonable inference.

Statement 2: *False* – There is no evidence of this in the text.

Statement 3: *True* – It is one of the stated duties of the perfusionist.

Statement 4: *True* – Again, this is clearly stated in the text.

Statement 5: *Cannot say* – Although this happens to be true, it is not stated in the passage.

Inferences An inference is something that can be assumed to be true or false because it links to, or is a paraphrase of, something in the text. For example, consider the two sentences below.

The train is stopping (STATEMENT).

We must be arriving at a station (INFERENCE).

This is a reasonable inference. However, train passengers know that trains often stop for other reasons (leaves on the line, signal failure, etc). In a verbal reasoning test, you are expected to make a reasoned judgement about these kinds of inferences.

A reasonable inference can be an indication of a *True* answer, if there is sufficient evidence to suggest this. If it is too broad an inference, it would be a *Cannot say* statement.

Assumptions You also have to beware of rushed assumptions. These can lead you to an error of reasoning. Although the previous text example states that a perfusionist is 'a skilled health professional', it would be wrong to presuppose that all skilled health professionals are doctors or anaesthetists.

As you might be realising, the ability to read and understand under time pressure is key to these types of tests.

Your reading speed

You might have heard of speed-reading. It can be difficult to know how quickly you read and whether you are really absorbing the information effectively. Your natural reading speed will be a big factor in how quickly you progress through the tests.

As a good rule of thumb, an average person can read at about 200 words per minute. Many students and graduates will have a higher reading speed. True speed-readers are able to read at 600 words per minute and above. This reading speed aspect is important in assessing how long you should take on each question. If you want to check your own reading speed, you can do this at WSJ speed-reading.[2]

Of course, the tests are designed to check your ability to work under time pressure and at the same time retain accuracy. Speed and accuracy is a fine balance. Some questions will ask you to read a passage of text of about a hundred words. If you have a reading speed of 200 words per minute, that will take you half a minute. You can then allow yourself half a minute to read the statements and decide which are true or false. Avoid, if you can, saying each word to yourself in your head (this is called 'subvocalisation'), as this slows you down. Aim to scan the sentences, allowing your eyes to move across each sentence. This will make you faster at reading. You will get quicker. Next is a more complex and longer passage. You can test out all of your skills, recalling what you have learned from the previous examples.

Verbal reasoning test 4 (200 words)

Decide which statements are *True* (T), *False* (F) or *Cannot say* (CS)

A common discussion point amongst media professionals is what makes 'news'. The most commonly agreed criteria for newsworthiness tend to be timeliness, importance or magnitude, and proximity. If something happens at a time that is right for you, is important to you and close by to you geographically, you are supposed to take notice and think that this is 'news'. It is, of course, highly reliant on the news reporter's own judgement of the value of the 'story'. How timely, important or close in geographic terms is that piece of news to him or her? This plays a part in how a 'story' is assessed for 'news' value. It could be argued that journalists may be the least suited to making these decisions on what is 'news'.

This rather selective perspective influences news creation and suggests that, by their careful selection of what is deemed to be 'news', journalists are at the forefront of what is 'media-fied'. Some would subscribe to the view that news is what the audience wants to hear or see or be more informed about. Opposing voices suggest that it is not so simplistic. The social media explosion, however, would suggest that media professionals rather than leading the news are riding on the wave of the news, lost in the tumult of the surf.

	T, F or CS
Statement 1: The idea of 'news' is a contested term.	
Statement 2: Newsworthiness is hard to judge.	
Statement 3: The media create the news through a subjective selection process.	

Chapter 5

Statement 4: Only journalists create the news.	
Statement 5: Social media news stories are solely created by journalists.	

Answers: Verbal reasoning test 4

Statement 1: *True* – This is a reasonable inference.
Statement 2: *True* – This is a reasonable inference
Statement 3: *True* – This is a reasonable inference.
Statement 4: *False* – This is not stated in the text.
Statement 5: *False* – The opposite is suggested in the text.

Advances in test design and scoring

Developing technology means that psychometric assessment is becoming smarter. Some ability tests can even tailor themselves to your skill level. Technology also ensures that scoring is fair. This is good news. Remember that recruiters are genuinely interested in uncovering your skills rather than trying to catch you out.

It also means you can't cheat, so don't waste your energy trying to find ways to manipulate your results. And don't ask someone else to take a test for you. Recruiters may ask you to retake a test at the assessment centre to check for consistency.

So you've had a go at some examples of verbal reasoning tests. You might have discovered your own shortcuts and strategies for dealing with them. Here are some ideas.

Winning ways

These are some useful approaches. Think about how they might work for you in a verbal reasoning text passage.

Strategy 1: Read each sentence, building understanding of the topic. Notice key words/phrases. There may be some unfamiliar words. Guess at what they might mean by the context of that sentence. *Extreme words* – Notice extreme words such as 'must', 'should' and 'don't'. *Generalising words* – Notice generalising words such as 'all', 'always', 'never'. These types of words often signal inferences in the passage. Go to the statements. Decide on those that are *True/False* first. Then decide the '*Cannot say*' statements.

Strategy 2: This is really a reverse way of approaching the text. Read the statements first *before* the text passage. Then read the passage with these statements in mind as a kind of sifting process. Try Strategy 2 on the Verbal reasoning test 4 (VR4). You will be familiar with the text, but this is just for practice. Give yourself 2 minutes for VR4. Time yourself. Check the answers again. What did you think of this strategy?

Strategy 3: Practise scan reading. Read a page of text, looking only for words beginning with 's' (or nouns, or words containing five letters). Quickly highlight them. This will help you to read faster. It will also train your brain to seek out specific information.

Strategy 4: Look critically at newspapers, magazines and web articles. Pick out the facts from the speculation and assumptions.

Strategy 5: Some assessment centres may include paper-based exercises, so be prepared. Take a highlighter pen with you to underline key words and phrases.

Reflection

Chapter 4 emphasised that just practising something doesn't guarantee that you will get better at it. Repeat the following reflection exercise after every practice or real verbal assessment you do.

Improve your performance
1. How did it go overall? What did I do well?
2. How was I feeling before, during and after the test? Did this hinder my performance?

3. What was I saying to myself? (It's normal – but unhelpful – to listen to your critical inner voice.)

4. Were there any questions that I had no idea how to tackle? What were they? How can I learn how to do them?

5. Did I manage my time well? What could I do to improve this?

6. As a result of this review, what can I do to improve my performance next time?

My story – Zain Shaikh, recent marketing management graduate

My advice, obviously, would be to try any practise tests you may be sent, as this will make you aware of the type of questions you will face. But this can lull you into a false sense of security, as the actual tests can be harder. I applied for loads of graduate jobs just for the experience. Many companies use the same tests, so once I'd done them a couple of times, I remembered how to do them and some of the answers.

Expect the unexpected – whilst many of the assessments used are the same, I had one which was really different. The questions were numerical and verbal, randomly interspersed with strange questions asking my opinions. Although it was tough, I actually enjoyed the challenge!

I had lots of rejections before I finally got an offer for two graduate schemes. I know people who gave up after two rejections. You just have to look at the statistics of how many people are applying, and don't be surprised when you don't get through . . . be surprised when you do!

Summary of best advice

Be honest with yourself: Are there things you know you need to get better at? Knowing what you need to work on is a great start.

Read every day: Read things that you wouldn't usually read. When you find a word (or sentence) you don't understand, look it up.

Be a 'truth detective': Find the facts and reasonable assumptions. Don't fill gaps in facts with your own opinions.

Read instructions: Make sure you don't fail an assessment just because you weren't sure what you were supposed to do.

Be calm and be quick: Reading and thinking under time pressure can be stressful. Take some deep breaths and focus on the task.

Reflect and learn from your experience: Every minute you practise; every assessment you undertake . . . they are all taking you one step closer to success!

Find out more

- **Test your vocabulary**
  http://testyourvocab.com/
  You can get an estimate of how many words you know. And perhaps you can take the time to look up the meanings of some new ones.

- **BBC Skillswise**
  http://www.bbc.co.uk/skillswise/topic-group/sentence-grammar
  This is a great website for adults who want to refresh their knowledge and understanding of the English language.

- **Learn a new word a day**
  https://www.wordsmith.org/awad/
  If you subscribe to this free website, it will send you a new word (and what it means) every day.

- **Kent University Careers Service**
  http://www.kent.ac.uk/careers/tests/verbaltest.htm
  There are really good examples of verbal ability tests on this website. They give you a score and explain the answers so you can learn.

- **SHL Direct – practice verbal tests**
  http://www.shldirect.com/en/assessment-advice/example-
  questions/verbal-reasoning
  You should definitely look at the examples and try the practice tests
  from this popular provider of psychometric assessments.

What to do next

Use the Thesaurus feature regularly. Try to expand your vocabulary
and understanding of words. Register on the Word a Day website.[3]
Learn to do cryptic crosswords so that you stretch your brain to deal
with strange word combinations.

Read fiction as well as factual books. These books use a wider range of
descriptive language. This can help you to build your vocabulary and
understand words in their context.

Take a look at this advice from a successful test candidate.

Observation by assessors

Contents

You're an alien on a strange planet. You're being watched. It's quite disturbing to be examined in this way. It's not the same as being noticed. It's the feeling of being scrutinised.

Assessment days have the power to trigger primal fears, associated with bad dream memories. Do you recognise these two common bad dreams?

- You find yourself naked in some public situation.
- You find yourself in an exam. You're completely unprepared.

Familiar? The fear of exposure and failure lurk in the dark shadows of a typical assessment centre day.

Being unprepared

Some applicants prepare for an assessment centre to some degree. They are ready for a primary school sack race. Others don't. They're hoping for the egg-and-spoon race. They used to be good at that. Most candidates need to be intensively primed and ready for the assessment centre assault course. If you're not willing to get in training, it will be just like turning up naked. You will be memorable, but for all the wrong reasons.

The unexpected

There's an element of the unexpected about any assessment centre. Most human adults hate the feeling of uncertainty. It can put you in a state of unsteadiness which destabilises your confidence. However, you should be given prior information about what to expect. This is often still quite vague, so it's normal to feel a bit unnerved by the prospect of an assessment centre. The best way to be protected from this confidence attack is to:

- Focus on your own talents and strengths.
- Research the employer.
- Become familiar with how the selection day will be organised so that you defuse any fear of the unexpected.

Your talents and strengths

Imagine that your talents and strengths are like a hand of cards that you have been dealt. If you want to succeed in this assessment game, you have to check the following:

- The cards in your hand (what you know you can offer).
- The rules of the game (what you know the employer is looking for).

Now you're ready to play the game. You need to play your hand in the cleverest and most convincing way. Have a go at the Assessment Centre Card Game exercise below, to get your head in the right place. You have a hand of aces. Each card represents an aspect of your personality, a particular strength or ability.

Self-assessment: Assessment centre card game

Think of examples of your personal qualities, strengths or abilities. These can be from hobbies, school, university or work. Here is an example of someone's hand of cards.

ACE	ACE	ACE	ACE
Quick learner	Good listener	Creative	Problem solver

Chapter 6

1. What would be your four aces? Record them below.

ACE	ACE	ACE	ACE
_____	_____	_____	_____

2. Based on your research into a chosen employer, what are their ideal criteria? Note down the four key things which that employer requires.

Employer research: What do they want?
1.
2.
3.
4.

3. Decide how well your hand of cards will 'play' in the assessment process you may encounter.

So, start by reviewing the match between what you have to offer and what the recruiter might be seeking. Record any gaps in your experience in the following table.

Self-assessment: Review	
1. Review the employer requirements (from your research).	
2. Identify those requirements that you fail to match.	
Employer requirement	Gap

Chapter 6

How can you find a way to demonstrate a better match of your attributes to the employer requirements? You might think of some of these ideas:

- Better examples from your experience that more suitably match the employer requirements.
- A quick way to pick up some relevant experience (e.g. some volunteering or through a study project).
- Doing some reading up about a topic like leadership or commercial acumen (two common requirements).
- Arranging some work shadowing with someone who has a role similar to that advertised by the employer.
- Finding a contact (ideally in that organisation) who could act as a mentor and encourage you to develop your potential.

Now come up with your own ideas to deal with those gaps.

Self-assessment: Ideas to fill the gaps	
1. Consider the gaps in your experience or skills.	
2. Think of a way to fill those gaps. Record your ideas below.	
Gap	Strategy to fill this gap

So, you have some ideas. Make a commitment to act on these. This means that you will be ready for the assessment centre event invitation.

The invitation

Recruiters will normally give a brief timetable of the event in the invitation letter. This can sound as much fun as a dentist explaining root canal surgery. Of course, it isn't meant to be fun. It is meant to be a rigorous process that lets an employer see you for real by assessing you through various tasks and tests. The timed activities, often detailed in the invitation, help them to know you by:

- Observing how you manage yourself
- Assessing how you think on your feet
- Finding out your abilities through tests
- Scrutinising how you interact with others.

So, you've done well to be invited to an assessment day event. Enjoy that glow of achievement. However, getting selected was just the warm-up. Now the game begins.

The assessment centre menu

Imagine being asked out to a restaurant. You'd want to know the type of food and the menu. What if you didn't know what to expect? Most candidates go to the assessment centre restaurant without much idea of what's on the menu. It helps to know exactly what each part of the day will contain. Think of this as the assessment centre menu. It's useful to think of it as 'Starters', 'Main Courses', 'Puddings/Sweets' and perhaps a 'Cheese Course' at the end. It's just like a menu, but you can't skip a course.

Assessment centre menu	
Starters	**Main Course** (any or all of these)
Welcome to candidates	Group exercise
Employer presentation	Team challenge
Plan for the day explained	Case study discussion
Allocation into groups	Role play
Icebreaker activity	In-tray exercise
Psychometric tests	Presentation
Puddings/Sweets	**Cheese Course (optional)**
Interview	Debrief/follow-up

The most usual 'slices'

High Fliers research (2014)[1] with graduate recruiters, found that certain activities were more likely to be assessed than others.

- 79% used group exercises
- 72% used presentations

- 46% used written exercises
- 45% used case studies
- 35% used role plays
- 15% used in-box exercises
- 7% assessed behaviour at a dinner or drinks reception as part of the assessment centre.

The day or half day is divided into slices, and the recruiters decide the make-up of each slice. You will receive a broad outline of what to expect in the invitation letter. It will look something like this:

Assessment centre plan of the day	
10am	Introductions and plan for the day
10.15am	Icebreaker activity in groups
10.30am	Psychometric tests
11.15am	Break
11.30am	Group exercise
12.30pm	Lunch
1.30pm	Interviews and written exercise (in parallel)
5.30pm	Finish of day (debrief)

The invitation might explain in detail what will be involved, or it might be a bit cryptic. Be confident enough to phone and ask for clarification if something seems mysterious or slightly ambiguous.

Being watched

The day is structured so that candidates progress through a series of assessed activities with military precision, with only short breathers or breaks. All candidates will be directed to the particular locations for these elements at exact times. You will need to be in a state of relaxed alertness and manage your own frame of mind.

You might start with a group discussion, then move onto a written test followed by a panel interview. You might have to give a presentation, do a role play or undertake a team challenge. (These will all be covered in detail in future chapters.)

However, there is so much more that is really happening. Throughout the day and even the night before, you will be observed. There will be two particular aspects to this 'surveillance'.

1. **Deliberate assessment of the required competencies:** Assessors will be required to notice particular competencies required by the job role and note these down.

2. **Instinctive judgements on candidates:** Assessors as human beings will subconsciously pick up impressions of candidates. They will aim to be objective, but their own subjective impressions will be shaped by the behaviour of different applicants.

What is being assessed?

You will be observed in the normal, everyday courtesies of the assessment day *and* in the formal assessed activities. You need to appear 'normal' and yet be aware that you are in control of the impression you make. You have to actively 'act' to present yourself to anyone and everyone you encounter. You are on show.

It can feel exhausting, but there is only one time frame for assessors to get to 'know' you. You have to make it easy for these observers to 'get' you. You either have to accept the rules of this weird game or decide not to engage (by not applying for employers who recruit this way).

Each activity will be designed to allow observers to notice and even uncover the particular skills, abilities, knowledge, experience and ethics of each candidate. These will be directly related to the job role and the person specification for that position. Each assessor will be working with a list of specific criteria related to that job role. An assessor *wants* to be able to observe these particular criteria or positive characteristics in action, through your performance in the different activities.

However, they will also notice any negative characteristics. What do you think might make a candidate seem unsuitable? Unfortunately, nervousness and lack of preparation really do interfere with an optimum performance.

Here's some advice about what not to do from Beth Jenkins (Shell Graduate Programme).

Employer's view – Beth Jenkins, Recruitment Manager, Shell International UK and NL

Candidates often slip up by:

Not quantifying their experience on their CV or making it specific enough:

Poor example – 'I worked for 2 weeks delivering a project which improved profitability.'

Better example – 'I worked for 2 weeks in a team of three, where my role was to develop a presentation that would recommend process changes to improve profitability. I delivered the presentation on time and to an audience of five, including the Head of Department. I made recommendations that would reduce overheads by 5%, and I know that one of my suggestions has since been implemented.'

Using purely academic examples in their interviews Shell UK receives more than 15 000 applications each year for around 150 roles, and all our candidates can cite academic experience, so it's best not to rely on this alone unless it is really going to make you stand out.

Not thinking deeply or broadly enough about a question Candidates may have applied for a specific career, for example Engineering or Finance, but we expect them to be able to think around each topic in a commercial way, looking at all angles and opportunities.

Not managing time effectively Try to practise e-tray exercises online, and ensure that for written exercises you don't spend too long planning and then not have time to write your thoughts down.

Not being authentic during the group exercise. Don't push yourself to be the loudest – we need candidates who balance exhibiting excellent listening skills with the ability to articulate their own opinions and ideas succinctly with impact.

Knocking yourself out

It can be like a knockout contest as you go through the day. Candidates might arrive for the morning part and only get through to the afternoon on the basis of high scores in the first activities. This sounds pretty brutal. As an applicant you have to focus on convincing them you are worthy of progressing through each phase.

The full-on 'extreme' assessment centre experience might mean that you are invited for 2 days to a venue involving travelling and staying overnight with other applicants and assessors.

Day 1 'winners' will proceed to Day 2. 'Losers' may be informed that they are not selected and leave after a half day or at the end of Day 1. This sounds like some confidence-zapping reality TV programme, but it is often a little more civilised. Nonetheless, the pressure of expectation and achievement cranks up the stress. Most applicants are nervy or pretending it is all normal, when it is anything but.

If the terms 'Winners' and 'Losers' offend you, the intention is to help you accept that the nature of these events is to select and deselect. Shorthand terms such as 'Winners' and 'Losers' are a way of desensitising you to the slight madness of the process. It is meant to be objective and thorough and yet may be based on subjectivity and random occurrences that no one can predict.

Here's a real example of this.

My story – Jack and the nightmare group member

Jack attended an assessment centre day for a prestigious national employer. Here's his explanation.

'We had 30 minutes to discuss a dilemma-type scenario and were expected to reach a group consensus. Most of the group were willing to cooperate. One group member was the candidate from hell. He dominated the discussion, talked over others and failed to take account of others' suggestions. I tried to put my idea forward, but this guy just belittled me and my idea. I didn't want to have a stand-up row but just held on to my temper. He wore us all down and gave his own decision at the end.'

Chapter 6

So what would you have done in this situation? It's a tough predicament.

In feedback from the assessor, Jack was told that he should have fought harder for his own idea, which had been the 'right' solution. As he had scored well in other activities, this ruined his chances.

The whole group failed, including the dominating group member. If Jack had been assigned to a different group, his performance might have been quite different and better.

Given that these 'out of your control aspects' are potentially part of a typical assessment centre experience, you can only focus on those things you *can* control.

Should it all go wonky, call yourself a reality TV dropout and move on to the next assessment centre, with experience under your belt.

Making the best impression

Things you can control

You might attend an assessment centre for a full day or half day, but some will require you to arrive the evening before. This evening gathering is a further aspect of the experience. It will involve a kind of 'meet and greet' on the first evening. You will meet your assessors and the other candidates.

It's worth thinking about how you will manage this stage of the process. It can be a bit disconcerting. You will realise that there is no time to relax. The show starts now.

Thinking ahead about this stage is enormously useful. To all intents and purposes, this is a networking event, an opportunity for you to demonstrate your sociability skills and ability to self-present.

Take a moment to think about what you can do to take control and make a strong impression. You might remember the beginning of university and the awkward first moments of meeting new people. Think about how you managed these start-off conversations. Can you think of someone who seemed at ease in these situations? What do you remember them doing?

Recall what worked for you and others, and apply that knowledge to an assessment centre 'meet and greet'. The next exercise will help you do this.

Chapter 6

Networking ideas: Taking control

You have arrived at the assessment event 'meet and greet'. The room is full of people. How will you conduct yourself?

Think of four practical things you can do. Note them down.

1.
2.

3.	
4.	

If you can, ask a friend to do the same exercise. Compare what you have written. What ideas do you both have?

Think of the practicalities, such as the following:

- Name badges
- Making your entrance into the room
- Getting a drink
- Handshakes
- Joining a group
- Balancing a drink in your hand
- Moving round.

So take a look at the list of key elements of networking success. Decide whether you agree with these ideas.

Key elements of networking success

1. Review your ideas from the preceding exercise.
2. Tick if you agree with the ideas on this list.

Networking elements	Tick
Rapport building	
Introductions and name badges	
Making a positive entrance	
Professional handshake	
Join a group of two or three	
Drinks courtesies and conduct	
Circulating	

How will these things be important? Use the following exercise to record your ideas about the significance of these aspects.

Networking practicalities: Why are these significant?

1. Think about each practicality on the list.
2. Note down your ideas of their importance for networking.

Practicality	Why this is important
Making an entrance	
Rapport building/ introductions	
Name badge	
Handshake	
Getting a drink	
Joining a group	
Balancing a drink	
Moving round	

So how did you do? The importance of these initial networking opportunities cannot be overstated. They allow you to:

- Show that you can interact in social events.
- Get to know other candidates ahead of any group activities.
- Get to know the assessors in an informal way.

Here's a summary of some networking rules.

The networking rules

Make a positive entrance Walk into the room with your head up and your posture alert. Scan the room for a friendly face.

Rapport building Be warmly welcoming to everyone. It will help you relax. Aim to find something you have in common.

Introductions When introduced, make a point of remembering people's names (see more in Chapter 12 on memory tricks). A simple way to do this is to say their name a few times once you have been introduced – for example: 'It's great to meet you, Sharon. How did you get here today, Sharon?' It may seem a bit laboured, but it works.

Name badge Position your name badge so it is on view, and try to spot others' name badges without getting too close and invading their space.

Handshake with eye contact Make sure you do this like you mean it. You should touch palm to palm and offer a firm clasp for just a second.

Make friends The other candidates and assessors are collaborators in your success, not the enemy.

Look for a group of two or three It's difficult to break into large groups. Find a smaller group and ask: 'May I join you? My name's Hafisa.'

Drinks etiquette It's often easy to start chatting to someone at the drinks table, but don't get stuck there. Make sure you have a hand free to shake hands while balancing a drink. It's courteous to offer to get someone a drink.

Move round This part of the evening might last for 30 minutes. Set yourself a target to meet six people. Break away from a group gently to get a drink, and move to speak to someone else.

Be memorable Pay attention to others, and 'disclose' something about yourself (something unique, but not too odd) to help them remember you ('Oh, I remember you said you went to Easter Island as part of your gap year').

Dinner with the observers

Try and seat yourself in the middle of a table where you have people on both sides. Normal courtesies apply with regard to table manners, but try to chat between small mouthfuls. Be careful to include all those on your table in the conversation. Continue to use the same networking tactics as before.

Alcohol may be worth avoiding, so you can stay alert for the evening and the next day. You don't want to risk any embarrassing, over-imbibing incidents.

Chapter 6

Overall, the 'meet and greet' can be a self-conscious experience, but it is useful to focus outwards on others rather than inwards on yourself. If you can direct your attention outwards towards the people you meet, you will find that people respond to you because you are genuinely interested in them.

The watching never stops

It is not possible to attend an assessment centre and not feel watched and measured. You need to prepare yourself by knowing the job role criteria and ensuring that you 'showcase' them. Here's an example.

Self-presentation: What would you do?

1. Read the details thoroughly.

The job role
You have applied to a private health care provider for a customer relationship management role.

Customers will contact this division to enquire about different levels of health care cover.

The organisation wants to recruit graduates who can:

- Offer a warm telephone manner.
- Explain policy details very clearly.
- Ask questions and deal with sensitive medical issues.
- Be professional, compassionate and ethical.
- Allow customers to make up their own minds.
- Be honest and genuine in explaining financial costs, benefits and exclusions to policies.

2. Now read what happens next.

Assessment centre dinner scenario
You are at dinner with a mix of candidates and assessors. One candidate mentions to you in a private conversation round the table that she has a mild form of epilepsy and that it can occasionally be triggered by stress, even though she takes medication.

Now decide what you would do. Record your response below.

Your response: What would you do?
_____
_____
_____

You might think that the above conversation is unobserved and random. In a way the response you give to this could be an indication of your own values. You might consider any of the following responses:

- Suggest to her privately that she could inform the organiser of the assessment centre for her own safety.
- Accept this as a confidential disclosure.
- Remind her that equality and diversity legislation will mean she should be treated fairly.

Now in this scenario, all three options above are valid. What if an assessor for this company overheard your conversation? Your response could be more significant than you thought. It could give an indication of how suited you were to the culture of that organisation. It might be noted.

In addition, this is the kind of scenario that you might be given to discuss in a group exercise on the assessment day itself. You need to demonstrate expansive and critical thinking *and* an ability to be ethical and work within legal guidelines.

Being authentic

The most common complaint by recruiters is that candidates seem to be artificial, even fake in their performance at an assessment day. Read what Luke Frost says about this.

Employer's view – Luke Frost,
Talent Manager, BBC Children's TV

It is a common mistake to pretend to be what you think the panel are looking for. Just be yourself! Be confident enough to convey your ideas to the group, and don't be distracted by those who are louder than you are. But be diplomatic enough to listen to others and make sure everyone gets their say. It's fine if you disagree with someone, but be constructive and diplomatic – often the best ideas come from a combination of viewpoints. Although we want you to complete the task/objective you have been set, we're also interested in how you work as a team member and how you relate to others.

Self-presentation

Most assessors, while expecting you to be presenting yourself at your best, want to see an authentic human being. So you will walk a precarious balance between being your normal self and at the same time aiming to show your best, in terms of what they are looking to see.

It is doable as long as you recognise how decisions are made about you, according to criteria determined in the job role profile. Research into the employer and the job role is time well spent.

It's useful to think about the way you present yourself (self-presentation) as a mixture of three main characteristics:

Thoughts: How you are thinking, how you are aware of your own thoughts and how you control them.

Behaviour: How you act and what someone else would see from you what you are doing.

Values: What is important to you in a given situation.

Take a moment to think about how you have performed in an authentic way in the past. What did you do to create this impression?

The next exercise will help you to analyse your own authentic self-presentation.

Self-assessment: Your authentic self

1. Think back to a situation when you know that you were completely true to yourself.
2. Note down in the sections below what you remember about your thoughts, behaviour and your values (what was important to you in that situation).

Thoughts	Behaviour

Values – what was most important to me

With some thought, you will notice that your authentic behaviour is driven by your values, predominantly. If you can focus on staying true to your personal values, even in an artificial and competitive assessment centre process, you will come across in a genuine way and make a good impression.

Consider what this major recruiter says about being authentic.

Employer's view – Klazien van Vliet, Early Careers Resourcing Director, Unilever

Throughout Unilever's selection process, I want to encourage all candidates to be themselves. Don't try to be who you think we are looking for. The selection process is as much an opportunity for you to assess if Unilever is the company for you as it is an opportunity for us to assess if you are the right fit for Unilever. Trying to be somebody else will never be as strong as being you. Being yourself will ensure everyone gets the most out of the selection process.

Being switched on

You are probably realising that there is a full-on intensive aspect to assessment centres. Think of them as an immersion experience. Make sure you do the following:

Research the employer: Know as much as you can about the company/organisation and the job role.

Maintain a good energy throughout the day: Take any moment you can to relax and breathe (use breaks; get outside if it is possible and sit on a bench; revitalise yourself with water, high energy snacks, a quick private yoga stretch, if possible, or whatever works for you).

Turn off your phone: You do not need that distraction.

Connect with others: Be warm and appropriately friendly.

Listen attentively to instructions and directions: Ask questions if you are uncertain about anything.

Be organised: Keep important paperwork, including the plan for the day to hand. Bring a pen and pencil with you.

Summary of key points

Know what you have to offer: Keep in mind what you have learned from the self-assessment exercise.

Research the job role in depth: Present yourself as the ideal candidate, matched to that job role.

Be ready to be observed and assessed: Expect that you will be watched and measured for your suitability for that job role.

Use networking skills: Demonstrate that you interact naturally with others.

Be your authentic self: Play to your strengths and present yourself as genuinely interested in that company or organisation and the job role.

Find out more

- **Prospects careers fairs and events list**
  http://www.prospects.ac.uk/events.htm
- **Guardian Graduate live blog**
  http://careers.theguardian.com/careers-blog/assessment-centre-guide
- **Warwick careers blog**
  http://careersblog.warwick.ac.uk/2013/01/21/making-the-most-of-an-assessment-centre/
- **The Student Room**
  http://www.thestudentroom.co.uk/
  Forums on many useful topics including assessment centres. Hear what candidates have to say.

What to do next

You can get a good sense of what to expect by reading the information provided by recruiters. Example case studies of successful candidates can be found on employer websites. Visit university career fairs, and speak to recruiters face-to-face. The Prospects website lists careers events and fairs at different universities and venues.

Assessment day – group exercises

Contents

The most common aspect of an assessment day is a group exercise of some kind. Remember that 79% of major recruiters (2014)[1] use a group assessment.

How it's organised

A well-run assessment centre is a finely tuned military manoeuvre. Candidates are moved from one place to another in an organised and speedy way. Some assessment centre days will have 50 or more candidates; others may only have 6. Whatever the number, there needs to be a constant flow from activity to activity so that candidates and observers are not hanging around too much. So how does the group-work part of the day work? Why do recruiters favour a group assessment?

The group perspective

You might be wondering why recruiters are so keen to assess you in a group exercise. It's obvious that employers need to know how you interact with others. However, the group scenario reveals so much more about candidates.

The observed group activity is, in fact, the closest thing to a real work simulation. Remember the CBI list of employability characteristics (2009)[2] (Chapter 1). You will notice that most of these attributes will be tested in the group work activities. You will have the chance to 'show off' your potential by demonstrating the relevant skills and attributes most often demanded by graduate employers. This will be the perfect opportunity to prove that you have:

- An ability to manage your own behaviour (self-management).
- The inclination to collaborate and cooperate with others (team-working).
- Interpersonal skills; that is, being able to interact with others productively: listening, questioning, clarifying, encouraging, and articulating your own views (communication).
- The ability to generate useful solutions or ideas (problem-solving).
- A proactive and constructive approach (positive attitude).

A rounded picture of a candidate

Graduate employers use well-designed group exercises which are actual simulations of the real work environment. It allows them to observe you in an aspect of the job role and determine how you would perform. Strong candidates will display the positive behaviours required by that organisation. You might find yourself:

- Arguing a point of view
- Persuading and influencing others
- Analysing the challenge or scenario
- Asking questions
- Leading the group in some way
- Managing the time allocated.

What is most evident in these activities is that enthusiasm, positive attitude and basic courtesy will take you a long way.

"Employers often comment that successful candidates are those who are ready to have a go at any exercise, who show genuine interest in fellow candidates and who participate actively in discussions."[3]

Group exercise basics

The most common aspect of an assessment day is some kind of group activity. In some ways, group exercises can be a relief. It's not just you against the assessment centre machine. Suddenly the cavalry has arrived. The focus is away from you as an individual. You can rely on others to help you get through this phase. The group will be required to work on a problem, a case study or a challenge of some kind. There's a time limit, but you're all in this together.

You might almost like this bit of the day if you enjoy team activities. You may even relax a bit because it's not all down to you. Being relatively relaxed is a good thing, of course, but you still need to be aware that you are in an odd situation. You need to work with others *and* yet you are also in competition with them. It is a weird balancing act. Take a look at this overview example.

A typical overview

So imagine this. You are assigned to a group of four and taken to a room. You walk in and see a table with some sheets of paper and four chairs. There are four assessors. You sit down and are given the instructions for the activity. You have an opportunity to ask questions. You are told you will have 30 minutes. You have to manage the time. Once the exercise starts, you cannot ask questions of the assessors. You are told that Assessor 1 is observing Person 1; Assessor 2, Person 2; Assessor 3, Person 3; and so on. Your assessor is sitting in a chair with a clipboard in a corner of the room, looking at you. Other assessors are positioned similarly to observe their assigned group member.

You will be facing your own assessor, but there will be a different assessor behind you facing another group member. This is what it

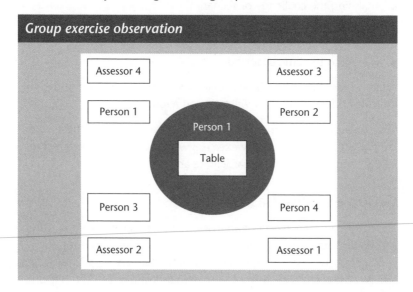

Group exercise observation

Assessor 4		Assessor 3
Person 1	Person 1	Person 2
	Table	
Person 3		Person 4
Assessor 2		Assessor 1

will look like. If you are Person 1, you will be facing your assessor (Assessor 1) with Assessor 4 breathing down your neck.

It can feel as if you are a bug in a jam jar.

What to focus on

So in this type of group scenario, it's normal to notice the assessor. However, all your attention needs to be on the group. Once you get started, focus on the group members. You will find that you have no attention left to worry about the assessors. You may see them in your peripheral vision taking notes, but all you can do is get on with the activity as set.

Although this may seem an unpleasant idea, it is useful to remember how curious and interested you were as a child when you put some insect in a jar. Assessors are the same. They want to know you and are keen to note down good behaviours they observe. These behaviours are the competencies that are required for the job role. These are marked on a scorecard (see 'Being Scored' later in this chapter). So get over the idea that this will be oppressive. They are paying you the compliment of real attention.

Types of group exercises

There are many variations of group exercises, and recruiters change them frequently. You will probably come across versions of the following:

- Icebreaker or short introduction welcome activities
- Problem-based or ethical scenarios
- A business or work-related case study
- Team challenges.

Many group exercises focus on a combination of problems, scenarios and teamwork.

Icebreaker activities

As the name suggests, these are designed to 'melt' the cold atmosphere and diffuse some of the natural nervousness that candidates experience. These are short activities at the beginning of the day. They may not be formally assessed, but they are a great opportunity to make an impression on recruiters *and* to get to know other candidates. A good start with these exercises will help your confidence for the whole event. Additionally, becoming familiar with other candidates might help you in later group exercises. Think about how you would deal with the three icebreaker examples that follow.

Icebreaker activity 1: How would you do?

Read the instructions below. Imagine that you are in a pair. How could you manage the time and remember the details of your partner?

Pairs exercise – You have 30 seconds each (1 minute in total) to find out some key information about your partner.

You must not take notes.

Aim to find out his or her name and two interesting facts.

At the end of a minute, you will be directed to join another pair and introduce your partner to this small group.

Your strategy

_____

_____

_____

Best advice The trick here is to start quickly. It's a bit like speed-dating, so don't waste time being hesitant. Look at the person, listen to him or her with great attention and make a link between the person's name and the two facts (see Chapter 12 for memory tricks). When giving your details to your partner, make your facts memorable because they are unique or surprising. It's your first chance to stand out, and it will help the assessor remember you if you can offer something interesting. Beware of seeming too mad or dithery, or of completing shooting yourself in the foot with an attempt at humour. Try this next icebreaker example.

Icebreaker activity 2: Five reasons

1. Read through the activity below, which was set for a group of five candidates.

> In your group of five, come up with five reasons for working for this company.

You have 5 minutes.

2. Set a timer.

3. Record your reasons below.

1. _____
2. _____
3. _____
4. _____
5. _____

Time issues

Even as one person attempting this exercise, you probably noticed that the time limit is a killer. Obviously, if you have done your research into the company or organisation, you should be able to come up with some strong reasons. However, in the group exercise there might be 25 reasons generated (5 per person), so there will have to be some speedy negotiating. Timed group activities are always problematic. Often groups are slow to warm up or they are so absorbed in the activity that they forget to watch the time. However, with a 5-minute limit, you really have to move fast.

Best advice Do some fast brainstorming where everyone writes his or her reasons on a sheet of paper. Record all ideas, and then vote so you reach a consensus. Aim to pick one or two that are impressive. For example, if the company has achieved great financial results recently or has been involved in groundbreaking research, these might be considered valid and impressive reasons.

A cautionary tale

Read Sam's experience as a warning.

Chapter 7

My story – Sam Scott

I went to an assessment centre at a major company. First, there was an icebreaking game where everyone was asked to write something about him- or herself, and then everyone had to guess which description matched whom. I wrote, 'I like naked rambling', which did not raise a laugh, just caused odd looks. I knew at that stage the whole thing was over.

Sam is a big confident character, but he underestimated what he needed to do in this first activity. He made himself memorable for the wrong reasons.

Problem-based scenarios

You will normally be allocated to an assigned group and know the time and place for this part of the day. There are some general characteristics of these group activities:

- You will be in a group of six to eight, typically.
- You will not know each other.
- You will be given clear, normally verbal instructions.
- There will be a written sheet detailing what you have to do.
- The time allotted for this could be 30 to 90 minutes.
- There may be one assessor watching each group member and/or assessors watching the whole group dynamic.
- All group members should contribute to the discussion, but different members might take different roles (e.g. as the timekeeper or the note-taker or the artist).

Here is an example of a problem-based discussion. Follow the instructions below the example activity.

Group problem-based discussion 1

Please read the following statement and then discuss this in your group.

'Big business is unethical.'

You have 40 minutes for this activity.

At the end of the 40 minutes, you will be required to present your group views. Each member of the group is expected to contribute to this presentation, for which you will have a maximum of 10 minutes.

Think about how you would approach this – your strategy.

1. What do you need to do as an individual?
2. How can the group best deal with this discussion?

Your strategy

_____

_____

_____

So how do you think you would do in this type of exercise?

Best advice Use the time factor to structure your discussion. It is worth suggesting to the group that you allocate segments of time for this debate. For example, you might suggest this time format:

Structured timings for group debate

1. 5 minutes – Define 'big business' and 'ethical' and 'unethical' – brainstorm.
2. 15 minutes – Discuss and explore the ideas and issues behind this statement (all the possible perspectives).
3. 10 minutes – Decide as a group the consensus view on these issues – which are the most important? (Take a vote if necessary.)
4. 10 minutes – Prepare the presentation and decide who will do each bit. Do a quick test run.

Ethical scenarios

When you are asked to discuss a business issue which has an ethical aspect, it is always worth mentioning corporate social responsibility (CSR).

This is a term used by many good employers to indicate their commitment to their local and global presence and impact.

Research into their CSR policy will give you a different perspective on that company/organisation. Remember, you will need to decide who will present each discussion point at the end of a group exercise. Aim to represent the view that is truest to your beliefs. Here's another problem-based discussion example with an ethical dilemma.

Group problem-based discussion 2: 'Lazy' colleague scenario

1. You are in a group of six candidates. These are the instructions for the group activity.

You have 30 minutes to discuss and decide what action could be taken in the given scenario. Be ready to present your group view at the end of the 30 minutes in a 5-minute presentation.

2. Read through the scenario below. Think about how you might approach this.

You work as a project manager in construction. You depend on the work of the quantity surveying team to keep your project on track. A colleague in that team is on the same salary grade and started on the graduate programme with you.

You have noticed that his timekeeping has deteriorated, and he is regularly late by 40 minutes on most days. This is delaying the early-morning team meeting and affecting progress on your project.

What do you do?

Best advice There is no perfect solution here. What is important is that you explore, as a group, all the possible reasons for this colleague's lateness. It would be hasty to assume he is lazy. There might be health or personal reasons for this lateness. Discuss possible ways of speaking to the colleague. How would you broach the subject?

The main thing here is to show balanced thinking and responsibility to take some action in a measured way. Alternatively, this type of exercise might ask you to write the script for what you would say and role-play it (see Chapter 8) instead of a usual presentation format.

Now take a look at an example of a group exercise involving a
business-related case study.

Business case study 1

1. Read through the letter of complaint below.
2. Think about how you might approach this.

Dear Ms Goddard,

We moved house recently. Your firm was employed to deal with
the legal process. We were quite shocked to receive your charges.
This is more than double what we were given to expect.

Please amend your fees and present us with an accurate bill.

Yours,

Mr and Mrs Brennan

So what are the key issues in this type of exercise? Firstly, it is a test of
knowledge for law students with regard to how they deal fairly with
clients. The Law Society is very clear about how solicitors should take
a client instruction, based on the Solicitors Regulation Authority.[4]
There's a high expectation of professional behaviour from solicitors.
The key areas that need to be discussed are:

- Who took the client instruction.
- The terms of engagement in writing.
- What was covered in terms of fee arrangements.
- The complaints procedure (and right to complain to the Legal
  Ombudsman).

However, then the group has to decide on a response.

Best advice Check the records of client meetings and instructions.
Follow the complaints procedure for that legal firm. Be prompt in
responding to the client, but check with a senior partner regarding the
wording of any emails or letters you send.

On the next page you will find another business case study group
exercise, based on a SWOT analysis.

Chapter 7

A SWOT analysis (assessment of strengths, weaknesses, opportunities and threats related to a business) is a fairly common business process, used to assess a company's continued success and progress.

Candidates for retail organisations in particular are often required to prepare a SWOT analysis prior to an interview or assessment centre visit. You might be asked to focus the SWOT on specific aspects of the business, such as quality, product range or competitor analysis. As a general rule, your research into any commercial company should take in the following:

- The competitors
- The product range
- Environmental aspects (green issues)
- Recent press coverage
- Mission/vision statements
- Social media/marketing campaigns
- Corporate social responsibility
- Growth, trends and profitability (Companies House)[5].

Business case study 2: Business SWOT analysis

1. Imagine that you were asked to do a SWOT analysis of a company, prior to the assessment day.
2. You are in a group of six candidates. You have 30 minutes.

Instructions:

Based on your research, discuss and share your SWOT analysis in the group. Prepare a 5-minute group presentation.

Give evidence of the strengths, weaknesses, opportunities and threats relevant to our business.

How would you approach this? Record three ideas below.

1. _____

2. _____

3. _____

So how would you do on an exercise like this? Remember, you would not be doing this on your own, and the 'group brain' can generate many ideas.

Best advice Use the time effectively. Make sure that all group members contribute ideas in the four SWOT categories. Aim to reach a quick consensus on the best ideas. Plan how you will present this. You will be confident if you have really done your research.

Team challenges

For some time, the most common group discussion was the hypothetical survival or adventure scenario. It's likely you have encountered this in your studies, as it's a very popular group exercise. The challenge aspect in this case is based on the simulation of physical survival and the team decisions made.

You may think this type of 'game' is irrelevant in terms of the job role. It's easy to see this as a lightweight exercise and not take it seriously. This would be a mistake.

This exercise requires you to work together, discuss issues and argue your case. It generally forces people to get involved and show how they can work together.

These team challenges are extremely revealing of how group members discuss, prioritise and show willingness to contribute positively. Have a go at the example on the next page.

Team challenge 1: Survival

1. Read the scenario below. Imagine you are one of the team of six who must discuss this scenario.
2. As a team, decide which six items you will take with you for the last climb to safety.

You and your friends find yourself up a mountain. The weather has deteriorated. It is late, dark and remote. You will need to get to a safer point, which will involve strenuous climbing. You have to leave some equipment behind. This is what you have at your disposal:

1. A tin opener
2. Six bottles of water

3.   Three bananas
4.   Rope
5.   A penknife
6.   A first-aid box
7.   Matches
8.   A torch
9.   A packet of chocolate-chip cookies
10.   A two-person tent
11.   A waterproof sheet
12.   A small bottle of brandy

3.   Which six items would you recommend?

Record the six items and your reasons

Item 1: _____

Item 2: _____

Item 3: _____

Item 4: _____

Item 5: _____

Item 6: _____

So which six items would you pick? How would you persuade other group members to your view?

Of course, there are no exact answers to this scenario. Each group makes slightly different decisions, based on the discussion. A real version of this could be part of a more physical team challenge where you have to use actual adventurous skills in an outdoor environment.

Remember, your final answer isn't that important. Your justifications and teamwork will be scrutinised and assessed. Your reasoning and behaviour is being put under the microscope.

Here's one more team challenge example.

Team challenge 2: Important global issues

Read the instructions below.
Imagine you are one of a team of six.

You have 10 minutes to come up with the 10 most important issues in the world today. You will present your list at the end of this time. You must justify each of the issues on the list.

So what would you suggest as the 10 issues? Test this out with a group of friends. It is surprising to learn how different people think about what is 'important'. There will be some common agreement issues.

Best advice Again the biggest problem here is the time pressure and how the group can quickly come up with 10 key issues. Here is a useful sequence to follow:

- Decide what, for you, is an important issue.
- Encourage everyone to quickly shout out thoughts, as it can help trigger new ideas from others.
- Mind-map ideas (Buzan)[6] as they emerge, and then get people to give reasons.
- Take the lead here without being bossy.
- Try to seek consensus.
- Be the person who watches the time and keeps things on track.
- Remember to leave 1 minute at the end to organise the list.
- Get the person who offered each idea to present the justification.

Reasoning behind team challenges

Exercises are planned for particular reasons. They are not random party games. For example, the global issues question will help recruiters know whether you are a globally aware graduate. You will demonstrate this through the following:

- Your knowledge of current affairs.
- Your awareness of the globally complex context that each company or organisation faces.
- The way you communicate your ethics and values.
- Your ability to influence others.

The globally competent graduate who can succeed in an ever-changing economic and political landscape is in demand (AGR 2012).[7]

Group exercises like this one allow a recruiter to assess whether you have the global graduate competencies required.

It's useful to analyse what might be behind any assessment centre group exercise that you encounter. Try to think beyond the obvious requirements. You should be able to guess at the reason for each type of exercise. They are all designed to uncover particular skills and abilities which that recruiter seeks.

Being scored

Depending on the activities, there will be a number of assessors, and each one will be assigned a candidate or candidates to 'watch'. The assessors will have paperwork to complete to show:

- What they have observed (against the defined criteria or competencies for that activity – see 'Scorecard').
- What they have recorded (behaviours and positive or negative indicators, shown by a plus or a minus sign).
- Their evaluation and score.

Here's an example of an assessor scorecard. The assessor will carefully record positive and negative behaviours, as listed below.

Assessor Scorecard		
Competency	±	Score 1–5
Interpersonal skills – listens attentively, asks open questions and makes suggestions		
Time management – keeps track of time		
Problem-solving ability – able to source a range of solutions based on awareness of range of issues		
Motivation and drive to accomplish task		
Overall score for candidate (out of 20)		Score

It can seem intimidating to be watched with this level of intensity. Try to think of it as the best chance you have to demonstrate your abilities.

Performance awareness

Whatever stage of an assessment process you are engaged in, one thing is certain:

> 𝘎𝘎 You have to perform. 𝟿𝟿

The one absolute for this process is that if a candidate does not 'show' a behaviour or competency or ability, he or she is deemed not to possess that ability. So you may normally be confident or good at teamwork, but if you aren't able to display these qualities on the day, you will be rejected and probably dejected.

You will need to be aware of how you are being assessed and take any chance you can to 'show off' the requisite behaviour. You might be uncomfortable with the idea of 'showing off'. Try to think of this as putting across a compelling demonstration of what you are really like. It does not have to involve talking loudly or taking over. The good candidates get the balance right by doing the following:

- Making good suggestions
- Asking good questions and clarifying what is required
- Involving others and helping others explore the issues
- Listening really attentively
- Inviting others to contribute by using their name (e.g. 'what's your take on this?')
- Being warm and encouraging
- Showing they are collaborative in style
- Taking responsibility for small details such as timekeeping.

Smart approach example

Lucy went to the group discussion assessment stage of an application procedure for a role in a charity. She knew she had passed the online tests. She wanted to do well in the group discussion. Here's her story.

Chapter 7

My story – Lucy

As I waited, another candidate arrived and came into the waiting area. We smiled at one another, and then he said, 'Are you here for the group discussion exercise?' I said I was and introduced myself and asked his name. We chatted. It felt easy and normal. Another candidate arrived, and we automatically chatted with her. Finally a fourth candidate arrived, and we repeated the same type of conversation. I think we were all a little nervous, and it settled us all down.

The great thing was that as we 'knew' each other a bit already and knew each other's names, we could hit the ground running with the problem scenario we were given to discuss. It went so well, and I think as a group we all made each other look good. It turns out we all progressed to the final stage, so it certainly worked!

Being watched all the time

Of course, professional recruiters will aim to be objective in the way they assess you. However, they will pick up tiny signals about candidates. These might be as inconsequential as whether a candidate shakes hands and smiles or disregards the queue for the tea. Small courtesies matter. So it is wise to stay 'switched on' for the duration of the assessment day.

Shine at group exercises

In general terms, group exercises assess three main competencies:

- Communication and how you influence others.
- How you connect with others.
- How you actively contribute to team outcomes.

So you need to be active in showing these characteristics. It may feel artificial, but you need to be more obvious than you are inclined to be, to show that you are listening, questioning, clarifying, organising and proposing solutions.

My story – Bethany McCrave, successful Unilever graduate candidate

Graduate schemes can be competitive, but don't let that get in the way of your judgement, especially in group exercises. Be assertive, but don't overpower your group. For the purpose of the exercise, other candidates are your teammates!

Employer advice

A meaningful contribution

Group exercises are an opportunity – a small window in time – to showcase what you can offer a recruiter. You will need to show a genuine interest in working for that particular employer, which is way beyond a cursory look at their website. Make sure you can demonstrate that you understand the vision and purpose of that company or organisation, its culture, personality and mission. Bear all this in mind when you are involved in the group discussion. Ensure your contributions are absolutely matched to that recruiter's goals and aspirations.

In the following advice, notice the words used that indicate the key drivers of Unilever. There is an expectation that candidates will 'share' relevant experiences in the assessment process to prove that their skills and abilities are a perfect match to that employer. Your contribution in a group exercise is one of the best ways you can do this.

Employer's view – Klazien van Vliet, Early Careers Resourcing Director, Unilever

Unilever is on a challenging journey to drive sustainable business growth, so we are looking for people who believe in our purpose to make sustainable living commonplace and who demonstrate the skills to lead in that context. Candidates who can **share real-life examples** of when they took on the role of a leader and realised opportunities they had spotted, or who find creative solutions for challenges they encounter, will stand out in our process.

Chapter 7

Summary of best advice

Introduce yourself and suggest that all the people introduce themselves quickly. Note down names on a piece of paper if you are allowed.

Call people by their name to involve them and acknowledge them – for example, 'I think that's a good idea Hassan'.

Watch the time and offer to time-keep or ask if anyone else wants to do this.

Finish a little before the end time, to organise the presentation or bring things together.

Keep the group focused on the task, but don't disparage others' comments.

Contribute by providing your ideas. Argue for them if you believe you are right, but listen to others as well.

Don't interrupt someone who is speaking.

See the group as a team that is working together so that all look good.

Ask curious and insightful, open questions (how, what, where, when, who).

Finally, it is worth realising that the group exercise is just one aspect of an assessment day. If it doesn't go as well as you hoped, be determined to perform better in another part of the day.

Find out more

- **Research companies** through Companies House (British limited companies)
  http://www.companieshouse.gov.uk/
- **Market intelligence reports**
  https://www.keynote.co.uk/market-intelligence/index
- **Kent University** – good website for business research
  Free publications http://www.kent.ac.uk/kbs/research/research-centres/ecg/

Chapter 7

What to do next

Spend some time doing some in-depth research into your preferred employers, the companies or organisations that attract you for a particular job role.

Chapter 7

Assessment day – other activities

Contents

An assessment day can be an up-and-down experience. Things can go well for a moment, and then something goes slightly less well. This variability can be unsettling. You might find you like one type of exercise and dread another.

For many applicants, the types of activities selected seem random and even mean-spirited. Unfortunately, there's a vague resemblance to those reality TV shows. You might reasonably think, 'Get me out of here!' However, despite appearances, it's not a reality survival TV show where you have to do anything to succeed. Recruiters don't try to create impossible challenges. The *reality* is this:

- Recruiters simply want to identify the best talent for their job roles.
- You have to help them by 'showing off' your talent.

What else to expect

Remember that the recruiter wants to see you from different perspectives, and so each activity is intended to allow you to demonstrate different skills and abilities. Some of the activities are very common. Some are less likely. For example, High Fliers research 2014[1] indicated that many recruiters assess presentations (72% of recruiters in survey). Nearly half use written exercises (46%) and case studies (45%). Thirty-five per cent used role-plays and 15% used in-tray exercises. Most assessment days feature a pick-and-mix of about three or four activities.

Getting to know you

Think for a moment about a photo of someone you really like. Most photos don't represent the whole, wonderful human being you know. In fact, often they misrepresent someone. An assessment day is the opportunity for an employer to go beyond the flat, one-dimensional view of a candidate, perhaps derived from an application form or CV. The aim is to see each candidate from multiple perspectives and to assess different competencies.

Different competencies

The different activities are used to assess the specific competencies required for each job role. There is nothing random about a good assessment centre. It will be planned so that candidates are offered the opportunity to demonstrate the competencies required by the role profile. Below is an overview of the most typical assessment activities, with a brief explanation. You already know about group exercises (Chapter 7).

Overview of typical assessment activities	
Activity	**Explanation**
Group discussions/ team challenges	A problem/scenario is given for a group of six to eight to consider.
In-tray/e-tray exercises	A hypothetical in-tray/e-tray is given. You decide what to do about different priorities.
Written exercises/case studies	A scenario or problem is described. You offer a written solution.
Role plays	You are assigned a role and 'act' out how you would deal with a particular situation.
Presentations	You present your views on a particular topic.

Have a guess as to which specific competencies will be assessed for each of these typical activities.

Assessment centre activities: Competency mapping

1. Look at the list of competencies below.

Competencies	
Oral communication	Teamwork
Written communication	Leading/motivating others
Influencing others	Ethical behaviour/integrity
Analysis/problem-solving	Dealing with stress
Judgement/decision-making	Organising/prioritising

2. Guess the competency assessed for each activity.

Activity	Competency
Group discussions/ team challenges	
In-tray/e-tray exercises	
Written exercises/case studies	
Role plays	
Presentations	

This mapping exercise alerts you to what recruiters are expecting in each activity. Here's a broad idea of what is being assessed. How does it match with your guess?

Activity	Competencies
Group discussions/team challenges	Oral communication Influencing others Leading/motivating others Analysis/problem-solving Judgement and decision-making Teamwork Ethical behaviour/integrity

Chapter 8

In-tray/e-tray exercises	Oral communication Written communication Influencing others Dealing with stress Organising/prioritising
Written exercises/case studies	Written communication Analysis/problem-solving Judgement and decision-making Ethical behaviour/integrity
Role plays	Oral communication Analysis/problem-solving Motivating others Dealing with stress
Presentations	Oral communication Influencing others Dealing with stress Organising/prioritising

Some competencies are generic and tested across all activities in an assessment centre. Each phase is designed to build a fuller picture of you as a candidate.

As you can imagine, most activities require you to be adept at problem-solving and able to think creatively.

Creative and critical thinking

Many of the challenges in assessment days can be managed if you can trigger your creative, problem-solving brain. The best way to do this is to resist the impulse to jump at one solution or to fixate on one aspect of a problem.

Be a creative thinker

You don't need to be artistic to be a creative thinker. It is a talent you can develop. It is more like a frame of mind. Creative thinkers train themselves to generate multiple ideas or solutions before deciding on one option.

Here's a typical creative thinking exercise. It will help you to stretch your thinking.

Chapter 8

Creative thinking activity 1: An ordinary object

1. Look around you. Pick out an ordinary small object (e.g. a pencil, a pebble or a comb).

2. Think of 20 alternative uses for this object. You have 1 minute.

Your 20 ideas (write them here):

So how did you do? Were you able to come up with 20 ideas? It's hard at first to think beyond the object's normal function. This is often referred to as 'functional fixity (Duncker 1945).[2] The same thing can happen when you consider a problem or scenario. There is a tendency to focus on an obvious or single solution.

When faced with a problem-solving exercise in an assessment centre (this could be a group exercise, an e-tray exercise, a written exercise or a role play), many candidates go for the obvious, almost their first response. It's really valuable to force yourself to come up with a mass of ideas or solutions in the first place. It helps you avoid limited, fixed thinking. It prompts a more expanded consideration which lets your brain be freer.

Come up with a quota

If you are doing this on your own or with others, a good way to start is to challenge yourself to come up with a quota of ideas, instead of just one. De Bono, the creative thinking guru, recommends this quota method (De Bono 1990).[3]

One big imperative is to agree, in a group or on your own, to avoid censoring ideas that emerge. The important thing is to free the creative mind. Let imagination rule at the start.

Once you have your quota of ideas, you can review them, delete some and weigh up options.

Try the next creative thinking activity. It might be a scenario you are given for a written exercise or a group discussion.

Creative thinking activity 2: Business scenario

1. Read the scenario below.

2. Imagine you are in this team meeting.

3. Come up with 10 ideas to attract more customers.

A team meeting is convened. The organisation is a TV company that wants to increase its customer base in the 20- to 30-year age group demographic.

Each person is asked to come up with 10 different ways to attract this audience.

Your 10 ideas

1. _____

2. _____

3. _____

4. _____

5. _____

6. _____

7. _____

8. _____

9. _____

10. _____

Chapter 8

Sensible versus creative thinking

Normal, sensible thinking would come up with the following list:

- Do some market research.
- Arrange a focus group.
- Analyse output that has attracted that age range.

Creative thinking might come up with this:

- Let's forget them and focus on the audience we have.
- Organise a programme-making competition for 20- to 30-year-olds, allowing them to write, produce and present their own output.
- Find out what they're watching instead.
- Broadcasting is over. Invest in instant streaming technology.

These creative ideas are not so special and may be less sensible, but innovation and invention often come from zany places.

It may be that you can use just a smidgen of this type of creative thinking in the challenging parts of an assessment centre day.

Critical thinking

In Chapter 3, you learnt about critical thinking for psychometric tests. It is really valuable to apply the same thinking skills to other activities in an assessment centre. Remember that critical thinking is highly valued in education and in the workplace. It is useful particularly for complex problems where there is no cut-and-dried answer.

It comprises particular characteristics:

- The process of thinking through a problem using reason as your guide.
- The intention to weigh up issues on factual evidence not hearsay or supposition.
- The willingness to be objective and fair in judgements made.
- A commitment to avoid bias and challenge assumptions.
- The exploration of multiple perspectives rather than one limited view.

The following process can be used to encourage your own critical thinking.

A critical thinking process

1. **Explore the issue, the data and the problem** by asking open questions such as *who, why, what, where, when* and *how*. Check the provenance of the data. (Where did it come from? How reliable is the source?)

2. **Notice any assumptions or inferences** (what you might be presupposing from the data) you are making.

3. **Ask yourself 'What else?' questions.** What else could this mean?

4. **Weigh up different possible opinions.** Rate each idea using a scale of 1 to 10.

5. **Make a reasoned judgement with a strong justification.** Ideally give your reasons and follow this with your proposed solution.

Try this simple critical thinking activity. You can use the process above to test it out.

Critical thinking activity 1: Newspaper article

1. Read and consider the article headline.

2. Suggest as many possible views for this incident.

3. Offer a considered opinion.

Headline

Four-year-old boy arrives at preschool with drugs and a knife in his backpack.

The Cantsfield Reporter (local newspaper)

April 1, 2014

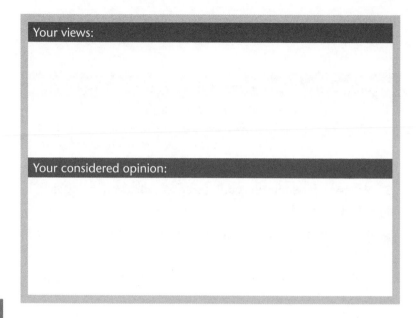

You might be aware that instinctively you jumped to a conclusion because of the 'startle' factor of the headline. However, if you engage in a moment's critical thinking, you will find yourself questioning the truth of this headline. There's a lot to consider. Your reaction will depend on the type of newspaper, its readership, the school, the drugs, the knife and so much more.

Here are a few considerations.

The date of the article – Could this be some April Fool's story?
The newspaper – Is this the kind of source that exaggerates or inflates a media story?
The drugs – Could this child need particular medication every day?
The knife – Could this be a plastic knife?

What kind of instinctive assumptions did you find yourself making? Being a critical thinker means training yourself to pause and consider beyond the obvious. How did you do? Were you able to control the instinct to make too quick a judgement?

Think about how both creative and critical thinking might be handy in most assessment centre exercises. It is especially useful in an in-tray type assessment activity.

In-tray or e-tray exercises

Imagine this: you have come into work and have been asked to cover for someone who is ill. You are asked to check their in-tray to see what is urgent or less urgent. It's a fairly normal situation. How would you approach this? Your approach could be quite revealing.

The idea of an in-tray may seem somewhat dated. Some people still use a physical in-tray and even an out-tray. What might be found in an in-tray? There would be random documents, bills, invoices, work in progress, requests for help and customer complaints requiring a response.

How would you decide what is important, trivial, urgent or non-urgent?

Making a judgement

Of course, it's a judgement call. In the absence of instruction from the owner of the in-tray, all you could do is take everything out, read it and put it into piles. In the end, there would be some that jumped out at you as 'urgent' or 'important'. You would deal with those first. Others could be delegated to someone else. Some could wait for a later decision. Others might seem completely unimportant, and you might decide no action was needed.

So for an assessment centre in-tray exercise, you could operate a similar system. Call it your 'do, delegate, delay' process. However, you would need to decide your criteria for what makes something urgent and requiring immediate action, especially when there seem to be competing priorities.

An e-tray exercise is pretty similar, but you are normally expected to do the same with someone's email inbox. The same process would apply. This is what an assessment centre version of an e-tray exercise might look like. For the real thing, you might have to record your responses on screen, in a timed test.

Chapter 8

How do you think you would approach this kind of exercise?

E-tray example 1: Decide the priorities

1. Read the brief scenario below.

2. You are required to assess the 10 items and decide on an appropriate response.

> A partner in your law firm is on holiday. You are a trainee solicitor. Here is her inbox. Decide what action needs to be taken. Give your reasons.

This type of exercise requires you to use your judgement and make swift but reasoned decisions. For a legal firm, graduates will be expected to come up with the 'right' answer in this scenario. You will be able to think of the 'right' answer if you have done your research into that company. You will understand its ethos and culture. For a legal scenario, you will be expected to offer succinct, well-thought-out, logical answers. Your reasoning will need to be balanced and well argued.

The next exercise gives you a taster of a typical e-tray test. Try the 'do, delay, delegate' sequence.

The 'do, delegate, delay' sequence

Have in your mind this sequence. It will help you in this type of prioritisation exercise. As you firstly scan-read through the emails, assign each inbox item to one of the categories. You need to detail the action you would take and write a written justification of your approach for each item.

E-tray example 2: The 'do, delegate, delay' sequence

1. Imagine that you have been asked to cover for a colleague who is on maternity leave.

2. Read through the email list on the next page. Assign each to the appropriate box below.

3. Give a reason for your chosen action.

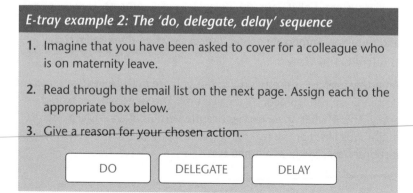

| DO | DELEGATE | DELAY |

E-tray example 2: The inbox

A. Message from HR
You need to book your appraisal with your manager. You will need to send out the 360-degree feedback paperwork in advance. It is overdue. Company policy says this must happen every 12 months.

B. Fire safety awareness training
This is mandatory training for all staff. Please comply with the staff guidelines and book onto the online course this month.

C. Meeting postponed
The meeting with the contractors arranged for May 23 has been postponed. Please can you offer an alternative date in June?

D. Royal visit
The Prince of Wales' office has contacted you regarding a visit to the company next year. They have not received a reply.

E. Disciplinary hearing for J Brown
You have been requested to attend the hearing to give evidence in support of J Brown. Please confirm your attendance.

F. Lottery win
Your share in the team lottery win is £100. Please let us know your bank details.

E-tray example 2: Your answers

1. List your decisions in order of priority.

2. Indicate by the capital letter from the inbox.

3. Give your justification for your chosen action.

1. _____
2. _____
3. _____
4. _____
5. _____
6. _____

Chapter 8

How did you do?

This might seem like the e-tray from hell, but it should help you realise what is required.

The prioritisation would probably go like this:

> **First: D** – Make a call to your line manager for an urgent response regarding the royal visit. Make sure that you receive a response.
> **Second: A and B** – HR should know this person is on maternity leave. Inform HR and suggest postponement for both at present.
> **Third: C and E** – Inform them that you are covering for your colleague and offer to attend in her place.
> **Fourth: F** – Report to the IT dept. This sounds like a scam.

Best advice To do well at this kind of exercise you need to:

- Focus, stay calm and take a few deep breaths.
- Use the time in a structured way. Read the instructions, and start with a quick scan-reading review through the items.
- Repeat the review, and decide the items that are 'delay' items.
- Then work down the remaining items and decide the 'delegate' items.
- What you have left should be the 'do' items. Decide an order of priority and a response. You might decide to send an email, but try to make it a call to action. For example, you might invite staff to a meeting to discuss a decision.
- All responses should have a justification – for example, 'I decided to arrange a meeting with the supplier to clarify the contract, because delay could cost us money.'

Prioritisation exercises of some kind are a common part of assessment days, but they could also take the form of a more detailed report in a written exercise.

Written exercises

These types of assessment exercise are a powerful way for recruiters to gauge your ability to analyse, make sense of data, make reasoned judgements and communicate clearly. They may also test your personal integrity, professional conduct and ethics. They can be in the form of a written report or a case study analysis.

Here are some examples from the health and social care sector.

These are career sectors where the everyday challenges are complex. Decisions have to be made which are sensitive to the needs of people in difficult situations. Creative and critical thinking are particularly useful for these assessments. Consider the following scenario. What would you do or say as this trainee health visitor?

Health visitor visit: Write a brief report

1. Read the brief scenario below.

2. What is your role and responsibility in this situation?

3. After this visit, what would you record? What, if any, action would you take?

4. Write a report of about 150 words, which summarises your opinion on this scenario.

> As a student health visitor, you visit a young single mother. She has a 6-month-old baby. There is a dog in the house. The house is untidy and the sink is full of dirty crockery.

There are a number of issues for consideration in this scenario. Whether you are a health care professional or not, you can guess that this has potential to be a child protection concern. Nonetheless, health and social care professionals have to walk a careful line. They need to make fair judgements of risk *and* demonstrate that they are being non-judgemental. Being judgemental is against the professional ethic for health and social care. It means that someone is making unfair, prejudicial judgements about a client.

In terms of the report for this activity, the question instructions suggest a useful structure. It suggests that a candidate should focus on:

- **The role** – What is the role of a student health visitor?
- **The responsibility** – What is the responsibility of a student health visitor?
- **Recordkeeping** – What needs to be recorded after any visit? What constitutes a risk to a baby?

- **Action to be taken or no action** – What is the judgement of this situation?

If the report included these four aspects, it would certainly answer the question. However, the judgement you make has to be grounded in the professional conduct expectations of that profession. Your research, prior to an assessment centre or interview, should take in the professional ethics requirements for that sector. Primary research talking to people in those job roles will help you know how to approach these situations.

In fact, some dirty plates in a sink and a household dog do not necessarily indicate an unhealthy environment for a baby, unless you have extremely high standards of hygiene. Jumping to a conclusion that the baby is at risk could jeopardise your relationship with that mother.

Ultimately, you would need to show balance in your writing. Demonstrate an awareness of exactly what your role requires as well as your responsibility in this situation. Similar issues are present in this next written exercise, which is typical of those posed to social worker trainees.

Chapter 8

Social worker trainee: A case study

1. Read the brief scenario below.

2. What is your role and responsibility in this situation?

3. Write a report of about 150 words which summarises your opinion on this scenario.

> You are a social worker trainee in a secondary school. A pupil mentions to you that his mother has a new boyfriend and that there is a lot of fighting in the house, especially when they have been drinking. He has two younger siblings who are also a bit upset by this. He doesn't want you to do anything.

So what would be the key aspects of your report? It's likely that your course of study will have prepared you for these safeguarding and child protection issues. Take the following Professional Conduct test to see if you have identified the key points. Decide which statements are appropriate actions.

Professional conduct test	Yes/No
1. Speak to the pupil's mother.	
2. Keep his confidence.	
3. Tell him that all families fight.	
4. Find out more about the fighting.	
5. Drop in for a visit to the family.	
6. See the nominated child protection officer.	
7. Make a referral to the child services team.	
8. Phone the police.	
9. Speak to your practice assessor/supervisor.	
10. Check back with the pupil after a week.	

So what did you select as the most relevant and appropriate professional conduct?

Here are the most appropriate professional decisions in an approximate order of action.

Speak to your practice assessor/supervisor As a trainee, that is your first course of action.

Speak to the mother (if your assessor allows you to do this) Find out more.

See the nominated child protection officer in the school You will be advised of the agreed protocol for incidents like this.

Make a referral to the child services team If this has been agreed as the considered course of action, take this step.

Scenarios and case studies are a common aspect of written exercises. The following examples are from a range of sectors such as law, business, retail, event management and teaching.

Chapter 8

Other written exercise examples

Law You might be given a client instruction task. This would require you to explain in writing how you would approach a meeting with a new client seeking legal advice. You would need to show understanding of what needs to be covered in this initial meeting, including terms of engagement; regulatory requirements; fee arrangements including money laundering protocols; and complaints procedures.

Business (banking/finance) You could be given a 20-page case study booklet with data and facts related to a fictitious company. There might be four questions to answer based on your reading and understanding of the case study.

Management consultancy You might be given information about a prospective merger of two companies, one of which had more established operations in China and Brazil. The task is to answer questions on staffing issues and plans for a smooth merger, taking into account a mass of emails, contracts and cultural sensitivities.

Retail Candidates are often required to undertake a 'mystery shopper' visit to a store before the assessment day. In the written exercise, they are required to comment on the location, the product range, price comparisons with competitors, customer service and recommended improvements.

Event management You might find yourself taken to a well-known hotel group and asked to write a critique of the venue as a potential location for a conference.

Teaching You might be expected to write a commentary on an article focused on a current or contentious issue in education.

You'll notice that written exercises are particularly focused on the job role and the typical work-related situations you will encounter. You can prepare for these best by immersing yourself in research about that employer. You will know what makes them tick. You will speak their language.

Take a look at a case study example below. Case studies are extremely common. They require you to read, critique and analyse information. They are used for group exercises or written exercises.

A case study example

Here's a more detailed version of a case study written exercise. It has an employment law focus. Read through the scenario, and guess at the key issues.

Case study example: Analyse the key issues

1. Read through the scenario.

2. Identify the key issues in this situation. What should you do or not do?

3. Give your 'best guess' opinion in the section below.

> You have worked for a small digital production agency for 4 years. You have developed warm relationships with clients. You have also successfully pitched for business. Currently £150,000 of the current business income is credited to your efforts and is producing on-going work. (The owner's business generation amounts to £50,000 in contrast).
>
> Many of your current clients have encouraged you to set up your own agency, indicating that they would rather deal with you solely. You have made the decision to hand in your notice and set up your own agency. You plan to respond to requests for work from any existing clients *after* you have finished working for the current agency.
>
> Your boss seems unconcerned at first when you inform him that you wish to terminate your contract. He becomes more difficult in your notice period and threatens legal action if you actively seek business from those he sees as his clients. He forbids you to inform your clients that you are leaving or to inform them of your new enterprise. Your contract of employment does not mention any restraint on your future employment, but does mention that you must abide by 'fidelity' expectations.

So what do you think are the key issues in this scenario? Aim to be objective and view it from all perspectives. Whether you have legal knowledge or not, can you guess what a 'fidelity' expectation is? In this situation, would you be restricted by this loyalty requirement? Think through this as creatively and critically as you can. Record what for you are the key issues and your considered opinion.

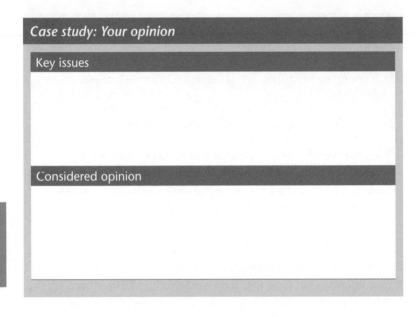

Case study: Your opinion

Key issues

Considered opinion

You don't really need to be a legal expert for this one. These are the key issues:

- What does the fidelity clause say?
- What does the contract of employment state?
- Can an employer put a limit on your future employment?

Most legal experts would advise that it is extremely difficult to enforce a fidelity clause like this, which obliges an employee to be 'loyal' to an employer for an extended period. However, it is worth checking a contract at the beginning of a new job role. Those employers that need to prevent client departures like this one often insist on a 'garden leave' arrangement within the contract (a paid period after the person has left, when the employee does not contact previous clients).

So when you have considered the case study or question, you will need to arrange your thoughts and commentary into a clear and concise piece of writing. Having a good structure for this is paramount. You will have a time limit, so a structure will keep you on track.

Structure your writing

Here is a suggested memory aid that you can use to structure your writing. It has the useful name of QUID.

QUID	
Q	Question – Rephrase the question at the beginning. Think – what exactly is the question asking?
U	Understanding – Show what you understand about the scenario or case study. Show different perspectives.
I	Issues – Identify the key issues. Explore them through discussion. Give a balanced critique.
D	Decision – Give your considered judgement as a final decision or conclusion.

Use this QUID structure to break up your report. Firstly rephrase the QUESTION, then show your UNDERSTANDING, then go through the key ISSUES and then give your DECISION with reasons.

After a written exercise, you may be required to present your decision (see Chapter 9) or act out how you might communicate this decision to a client or customer. These role plays demand the most creativity and often deliver the most stress.

Role-play exercises

The use of role play is a way of simulating the real competencies required in the job role. So, for example, trainee doctors may have to role-play a consultation with a patient. Similarly, police trainees might have to deal with an actor playing a difficult member of the public. There are myriad role-play scenarios, but typically it might involve one of the following:

- Acting as you would for real with a difficult customer.
- Writing a script related to an incident and delivering it.
- Interacting with an actor who acts the part of a customer/client.

A role-play example – how would you do?

Consider the following brief and plan out how you would approach this.

> ### Role play: Prepare for this meeting
>
> You are the manager of a small interior design company. A client commissioned a design brief for restaurant premises. The project design and costings were sent to the client with a bill. The client responded by email. The design was not to her liking, and she felt the bill was premature. She demanded a meeting, as she was really unsatisfied with the lack of consultation in the design process. She had expected that billing for the work would follow her approval.

Best advice Firstly, think what you would want to say to the client. Prepare a script for what you want to say. Apologise early on for the misunderstanding. You want to retrieve the situation by building a better relationship.

One of the slightly stressful aspects of these role-play-type activities is the expectation from the assessors that you behave normally whilst having to 'act out' something.

Ways to be successful at role-play scenarios

Very few people like the idea of acting something out. It feels false and a bit weird. However, this type of exercise is asking you to predict how you would behave in certain scenarios, so it's actually 'real play' rather than role play. Most people who do well at role play, find that focusing on the scenario *as if it were for real* helps them frame it in a useful way. There are some other ways to make it a better performance:

1. **Read the scenario** two or three times. There will be clues to help you predict the behaviour of the other person.
2. **Prepare a script** – just a few words and phrases.
3. **Apologise** if something has gone wrong, even if it does not seem to be your fault (as the role-play character).
4. **Show interest** and ask questions.
5. **Agree action** at the end.

Chapter 8

Finally, take a look at some less predictable challenges which recruiters may spring on you.

Unusual challenges

Whilst most organisations or companies tend to use mostly standard assessment exercises, there are some, particularly in the creative, media and marketing industries, that are surprising or even bewildering. Here are some examples.

A speed research activity

A theatrical agency posed the following challenge to shortlisted candidates:

'You have 1 hour to find out the favourite food of a famous TV chef.'

So what would you do in this situation?

While most people think of doing a Google search, it may be that there are other quicker ways to find this out. What other ways might work? You might be able to use Facebook or Twitter to put out a call for help. You might know someone who knows someone in TV. You might be able to phone a library or a catering college.

Social media confidence

Other companies want to see how social media aware you are and might give you a Twitter challenge. Some are interviewing through a series of Tweets or a 'Twitterview', or they're expecting you to apply for jobs through a 10 Tweet CV or 'Twesume'. It might seem really cheesy, but it's worth realising that recruitment practices change and move fast.

A quick draw game

Imagine you were asked to communicate your personal motivation and determination through a drawing on a flipchart. How would you do this? What symbols and images would you use to communicate this? Candidates and assessors would have to guess your message. This was used for commercial candidates (not creative design applicants). Try this now on a spare sheet of paper.

The real point here is that you can, to a degree, be prepared for the unexpected. You can guess that any unusual challenge will be related to that job role and that industry. Make sure you are fully knowledgeable about that industry or sector. Then you will be at least partly ready for any surprises.

Finally, here are some thoughts on assessment centres from someone who went through and succeeded. Notice it might end up being a regular event in your career.

My story – Chloe Hutchinson, Buyer, Tesco 'Florence and Fred'

Within my company an assessment day will happen several times throughout your career. The first assessment day I did, I was dreading really, but came out of it feeling it was much easier than I thought.

The good thing is you can prepare well for most parts of it, even looking up types of group exercises that could be used – and working out what assessors are looking for. But I know going through a day like this will show the company a rounded picture of me. It's a fair process and works well, I believe.

Find out more

- **Michael Page**
  http://www.michaelpage.co.uk/our-expertise/retail/retail-assessment-centres
  Advice on performing at assessment centres.
- **University of Kent Careers Service**
  http://www.kent.ac.uk/careers/interviews/role-play-interviews.htm
  Advice on role plays.
- **University of Edinburgh Careers Service**
  http://www.ed.ac.uk/schools-departments/careers/using-careers-service/cvs-apps-interviews/assess/types-exercise/in-tray
  Advice on in-tray exercises.

What to do next

Try out the in-tray and written exercises available through the websites.

Do some friendly peer-to-peer coaching for role plays. Make a video of yourself, and review your performance. Decide how you can improve your ability to be convincing in role plays. Use the QUID structure for a written scenario.

Chapter 9

Presentations – prepared or unprepared

Take a poll of 10 friends. Find out who actually likes delivering a presentation. You'll be lucky to find three who enjoy the experience. So why does the requirement to deliver a presentation have such a bad vibe?

A different mode of communication

Every day you communicate with people. You present information, share ideas, persuade and even inspire them. Being a presenter is simply a familiar mode of communication with a difference. It's a natural extension of what you do every day. So when you're asked to present on a topic in your studies, for work or job applications, it should be as easy as breathing. So why does it suddenly feel strange, awkward, unnatural?

Spontaneous presenting, the everyday stuff, is normal because you don't think about it. You go out into the world and present yourself and that's it. Occasionally, these presenting communications go wrong because you have not planned out what you want to say. Generally though, they go well. So planned presenting ought to have the benefits of natural everyday presenting with the benefits of some planning.

What makes it difficult?

There must be something else that makes presenting problematic. Many people hate delivering presentations. So what's this presentation angst all about?

It seems that being asked to deliver a presentation can trigger some illogical fears. Consider the list of common fears below. You probably recognise some of them.

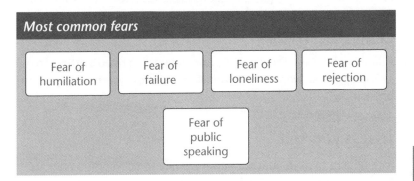

Most common fears

| Fear of humiliation | Fear of failure | Fear of loneliness | Fear of rejection |

Fear of public speaking

Of course, these fears are irrational. Nonetheless, the physical symptoms of any irrational fear are compellingly convincing. Your body may go into shutdown mode. Any number of horrible or panicky feelings may assail you.

Research shows that many people actually fear public speaking more than death. It is the top fear (Psychology Today 2012).[1] It is also an unpleasant package of the other common fears. When you give an assessed presentation, there is unfortunately the risk of failure, humiliation, rejection and even loneliness. The loneliness comes from that sense that you are on your own as the presenter and not part of the group.

Overcoming the fear

If it seems like a fearful event to you, it's time to deal with this fear storm. Start by becoming aware of your typical mindset when faced with delivering a presentation. Consider how you think about presentations. You may notice that any fear or foreboding is predominantly triggered by your thinking. Here's some typical thinking:

'It's going to go wrong.'   'I'm going to embarrass myself.'
'No one will like me.'

Chapter 9

This catastrophic, or 'stinking thinking', (Altiero 2006)[2] can be debilitating. Think of it as an act of self-sabotage. It can make you unable to perform in a natural, genuine way. It's as if you have become someone else – a nervy, frozen impersonation of your true self.

Interviews and assessment centres are likely to be *fearful* for many candidates. You may have delivered reasonable presentations as part of your studies. Delivering a presentation as part of a selection process for your first graduate job will add to the stress levels. You need to find a way to move up a gear and defuse these irrational fears.

Change your thinking

Changing how you think about presentations is a good starting point. This chapter will work on your thinking and show you how to perform brilliantly.

Assess yourself

It's useful to think about your current ability to deliver presentations. How would you rate yourself against a really good presenter?

Take a moment to think about the characteristics of a really good presenter. What techniques would this person use? Try to remember watching a good presenter. Analyse the performance.

Note down the characteristics in the following table. Then think of your own typical presentation performance. Which of those characteristics do you have? Which techniques do you use?

Self-assessment: Good presenter comparison

1. List the characteristics/techniques of a good presenter in the left column.
2. Tick the right column if you have, at any time, demonstrated these characteristics or techniques.

Good presenter	You

Most people recognise that good presenters display particular knowledge, attitudes, skills and behaviours. Your list might have included the following:

- Confidence about the topic presented – knowledge
- Positive and enthusiastic – attitude
- Humour as appropriate – attitude
- Clear, structured message – communication skill
- Movement, posture, eye contact, voice projection, audience engagement – performance skill/behaviour/technique.

You probably have a clear idea of what makes a good presenter. This means that you are part of the way to being good yourself. Don't worry if you failed to tick any of the boxes. You have clarified what you need to do to be better at presentations.

What is being asked of you

The invitation letter

Here's a sample letter inviting a candidate to an interview.

5 May 2014
Re: Application for role of PR assistant

Dear James,
Thank you for your application for the above role. We are delighted to offer you an interview. Please attend on 23 July 2014 at 10am at the address above. Please allow 2 hours for the process.

Yours sincerely,
Django Richards
Managing Director

Chapter 9

So on the face of it, this seems just like a standard interview and that's what the applicant thought. Here's his story.

My story – James

On arrival I was told that my first interview would be with the Executive Assistant to the MD. Next, I had 20 minutes to prepare a 10-minute presentation on a fictitious food product. I quickly drew a grid on a piece of paper – divided it into five separate 2-minute sections and scribbled an idea in each section.

What surprised James was the requirement to deliver a presentation without any prior warning. The '2-hour' mention in the letter might have made him think that it would be more than an interview, but it was still a little unnerving. The point here is that the invitation letter may not fully alert you to what will be required. You have to be ready for the unexpected unless the letter is very specific. It would be advisable to contact the company ahead of the interview if it is unclear as to what will be required. In fact, you might score points for asking for clarification.

Plan the presentation

Take a look at the plan which James used. Notice how he broke up the time slot into 2-minute chunks.

Example presentation plan	
Intro	Topic – new exotic fruit from Mauritius – low calorie and sweet. What the nutritionists say about it – how it was discovered. Screwed-up piece of paper in shape of fruit to approximate size.
Point 1	Marketing push for this fruit through retailers and slimming organisations. It tastes great (market research).
Point 2	Product direct from growers – more jobs for that part of the world.
Point 3	When you want to reach for a 300-calorie chocolate bar, try this instead.
Ending	People are in search of something new to eat. They will love this.

So what do you realise from James' story?

It is clear that the element of surprise (it was more than just an interview) was part of the interview process. In fact, what James experienced was a mini assessment centre. He had to contend with his own reaction to the 'surprise'. He was able to manage his own performance by swiftly drawing up a plan. This plan included:

- A visual aid (the fruit made of paper)
- Some interesting 'made-up' facts
- The basics of a script made up of key words and phrases.

He focused on designing the presentation and was not thrown off stride by the surprise element. How would you have reacted?

Surprise presentations

James was able to regulate his own nerves and performance through a structured and analytical approach. The 10-minute presentation structure is easily constructed with five chunks. Without PowerPoint® or visual aids, he did well to create a visual aid (the screwed-up paper in the shape of the fruit). This took the focus off him for a while and showed a degree of inventiveness. He would not have been able to deal with the surprise without a solid base of knowledge about the company and its business sector.

Better research

So here's what to do to prepare for the unexpected:

Primary research Track down someone who works for that organisation. Ask friends and family if they know someone who works there. Get in touch with these contacts, and ask if you can 'pick their brains' about the company. Find out some interesting, less well-known facts.

Social media research Set up a Google alert so that anything current about the company turns up in your email inbox.

Follow/'like' their LinkedIn and Facebook pages. Use LinkedIn. This is a professional profile space where companies and individuals present themselves. Many recruiters use LinkedIn to vet and source applicants.

Start with the LinkedIn company page and see who is listed. Check if you can access the contact details of any company representatives. Find out if they belong to a 'group' on LinkedIn, and join that group. Make contact in some way, and ask if you can book some time for a quick chat.

Secondary research Do an online newspaper search using that company name as a key word. Find a friendly university librarian, and ask for help to search company information databases. Using more than one search engine, try different key words for that industry or sector. Find out about the current trends, issues and challenges. Save relevant articles. Analyse the themes from this data.

Most candidates do a Google search and check the organisation or company website. Aim to go beyond this normal approach. If you have done all the above, you will give yourself a fighting chance for the surprise presentation challenge.

Having received the invitation letter, be brave enough to clarify what is expected if it is a bit mystifying. Phone up and ask questions so that you know as much as possible. If they are prepared to share this, find out what equipment you can use, whether you can use a programme such as PowerPoint, who will be the audience, the timings, and the room location and size.

If you have to design and deliver a presentation unexpectedly, it's useful to test out the surprise presentation structure.

Speed-design a presentation

Let your creativity flow within a defined presentation structure like the one that follows. Have a go now. Pick from the following three topics. You have 10 minutes to create a 5-minute presentation on your favourite music, food or sport. Use the plan given here.

Basic presentation plan

1. Use the structure below to plan out your 10-minute presentation.
2. Try to incorporate a visual aid of some kind, an interesting fact and some key words for your script.

Chapter 9

Your presentation plan on ...	
Intro	
Point 1	
Point 2	
Point 3	
Ending	

How helpful was it using this simple, structured approach? Practising beforehand like this for surprises can make it all seem less surprising.

Prepared presentations

Fortunately, many employers will not spring a surprise on applicants. Below is an example of how an applicant was forewarned of what to expect.

25 June 2014
Re: Application for role of Chemist

Dear Siobhan,
We would like to invite you to attend an assessment process for the role of chemist on 23 July at 2 p.m. at our head office in Cheeping.

You will be required to deliver a presentation lasting 10 minutes on **What customers need to know about our nutritional products.** This is the format for the event.
2 p.m. – You will be shown round the labs with other applicants.
2.30 p.m. – You will deliver a presentation to other applicants and four assessors.
3 p.m. – You will be interviewed by a panel of staff including the head chemist.
Please confirm that you will be attending, and feel free to phone me if you have any further questions.

Yours sincerely,
Django Richards
Managing Director

This is more normal in terms of recruitment practice. Knowing your topic in advance is clearly an advantage. However, the recruiter will have greater expectations of you. Your research will really give you the edge.

Different recruiters will require you to present on different topics according to the particular employer and job sector. Here are some examples.

Presentation topic examples

These are just a flavour of the kind of presentation topics.

- **Retail** Deliver a 10-minute presentation on fashion trends for next season.

- **Business** Pick an article or feature from the *Financial Times* that is relevant to our company. Present recommendations to the managing director.

- **Environmental consultancy** Suggest some ways that a company can become 'greener'.

- **Pharmaceutical sales** Persuade the panel of the merits of a new drug for dementia (data provided).

- **Hospitality management** (international hotel group) What will be your main focus in this role? How will you measure success?

- **Computing** Tell us about a product or service we offer that impresses you.

- **Food industry** Give a business decision on the merits of endorsing the healthy living recommendations of the government.

- **Engineering** Present your final year project from your degree. How did this develop you for this role?

It's actually easier than you might think to deliver a standard, informative presentation, especially if you use a good structure and do your research. However, there are some extra ingredients that good presenters use. These can turn a good presentation into a great one.

Recruiters are likely to watch six to eight presentations in a day on the same topic. Make sure that your presentation is memorable.

Moving it up a gear

So you have a basic structure for your presentation. What would make it even better? Here are some extra ingredients that good presenters use. They add freshness to a formal or informal presentation.

Look at the list below of possible additional aspects you could utilise. What do you think would be beneficial?

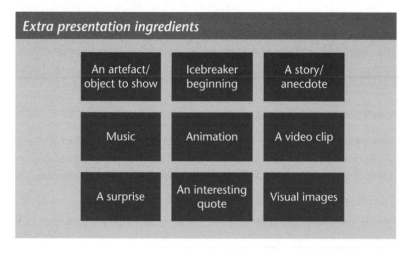

Extra presentation ingredients

An artefact/object to show	Icebreaker beginning	A story/anecdote
Music	Animation	A video clip
A surprise	An interesting quote	Visual images

Now obviously, your choice of extra ingredients will be informed by your topic and your research into that company or organisation. It is unlikely that you will use a piece of rock music as an intro when presenting to barristers' chambers. However, if you are a youth worker trying to show how you would motivate teenagers, a rock music intro could be very appropriate.

Here are some ideas for you to consider. Read through the explanations, and think about how you might use these.

Extra ingredients

Artefacts Perhaps you remember 'show and tell' at primary school. You were asked to bring something interesting from your holiday and talk about it. This is a great way to engage the audience. A trainee teacher could bring a collection of buttons or shells or objects relevant to the lesson topic. A banker could bring some fake bank notes. An architect could bring a tower made of wooden building blocks. These act as a visual aid focus.

Remember, the artefact has to be broadly relevant or linked to all or some part of your presentation. Irrelevant artefacts will just puzzle your audience. Artefacts can be used as a good icebreaker.

Here's another example. An applicant for an actuary graduate role might bring a child's abacus as an artefact. He might use it to emphasise that risk analysis these days is more complicated than basic counting but still must be accurate and useful (like an abacus).

Visual images Many presenters use some kind of slide presentation (PowerPoint or similar). However, if the audience has to focus on reading crammed text on slides, they are not listening to you. They are also likely to doze off. So try to use visual imagery to put your message across. A small graph or flow chart or the right photo can really be effective.

Here's a really simplistic example.

A presenter wants to surprise the audience. She wants to tell them that the British are not a nation of dog lovers. In fact, they prefer cats, based on a recent survey. (This was probably undertaken by a cat food company.)

The presenter could explain this with accompanying text on a slide. It would show something like this:

Dogs versus cats

'Cats are the most popular pet in the UK. Dogs are not as popular as people think.'

This could be shown in a more visual way.

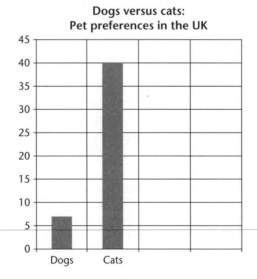

**Dogs versus cats:
Pet preferences in the UK**

It might seem a bit obvious, but think about how you could make better use of visual images or graphs in your presentations.

Icebreaker/Story/Quote/Surprise You will formally introduce yourself, but it is useful to have something that warms the audience up and engages their curiosity. Your artefact might do that, as would a clever quote, a story or a suitably humorous anecdote.

Anything that surprises an audience is valuable. Remember, this poor panel might have to sit through days of presentations. You have to stand out.

Music/animation/video clip All these can work, but you need to think through whether the time will allow for these, whether you will need a good Internet connection and whether they will add value or be a distraction to the presentation.

Presentation slides

You might use a PowerPoint format or even a Prezi,[3] which is a more dynamic presentation. Keep to about a slide per minute as a maximum (five slides for a 5-minute presentation). Keep the slides simple, with one picture and one line of text. Don't let the slide do your talking. It should act as a prompt. Make sure your name is on the first slide and 'Any questions?' is on the last slide.

However, you don't have to use PowerPoint or Prezi. You can do it 'naked' without any technology input (but with your clothes on!). Presenting without the use of a screen and computer can be quite liberating. You could draw something on a flipchart and bring it along or use an artefact as the focus.

The best thing about using a prepared presentation format like PowerPoint, is that you can print the notes page for yourself and as a handout for your audience (to give out as a memory jogger afterwards, to help them remember you).

Be the audience

If you can hypothetically transport yourself into the seats of the audience and imagine what they want to hear, what they want to know, what would be most interesting to them, you will be coming from the right perspective in designing the content of your presentation.

Select the most exciting content

Think about the most exciting point you want to make. This is probably what you want them to *remember* from the presentation, what Andy Bounds calls the 'take-away'.[4] What do you want the audience to 'take away'? What will make this memorable?

Employer's view – Peter Jones, graduate recruiter

Graduate Recruitment Presentations

It seems obvious but a presentation needs to be:

- Structured (have a beginning, a middle and an end).
- Clear in its objective.
- Timed perfectly.

As the presenter, don't just read it out (from the screen).

The test of a good presentation is this: Have the observers learned anything? Did they feel involved, or were they just bored?

My overriding tip would be: 'Just make it interesting!'

Designing the presentation

A presentation challenge

This is a bit like paint-by-numbers, but it is useful to try and design a presentation in this way. Follow this sequence.

Decide your goal What do you want it to achieve? What question do you need to answer?

Research the topic Find out everything you can.

Think of the audience What will they want to know? What will make it exciting and informative for them?

Icebreaker introduction Think of a way to get off to a good start. Use a surprise fact or a statistic or a quick anecdote relevant to the topic.

Resources Think of what you will need to use. Do you want to use slides or a flipchart or a poster? Do you need a music clip or animation? What else will you need to bring the presentation to life?

Work out the timing Think about what is possible in the given time limit.

Decide the main four to five key points Be selective. Based on your research what are the key messages you want to communicate?

Select the most interesting detail What is your most surprising or valuable point? Place this in the middle of your presentation. This is when audience attention dips.

Plan the final section Decide your concluding remarks. Aim to finish on an upbeat note.

Now create a compelling presentation. The template primes you to think of all the ingredients you will need.

Design a compelling presentation	
Note down on the right your beginning ideas for all the sections.	
Goal	
Research	
Audience	
Icebreaker	
4 or 5 key points	
The best point	
Plan the ending	

Delivery with impact

The actual delivery of your presentation is probably even more important than the content. You have probably sat through beautifully structured, cleverly worded presentations that turned you into a zombie because of the boring delivery. Concentrate on two key aspects in terms of the performance:

- Your physiology – that is how your face, eyes, posture and hands are delivering the non-verbal messages of your presentation.
- Your tonality – how you are using your voice, the pace of speaking, the volume and projection.

Remember the good presenter comparison you did. Now do something similar, thinking particularly about the presenter's physiology and tonality. Map out what was noticeable about this person, specifically based on these non-verbal aspects, which are powerful communication channels in their own right. Note down your thoughts in the next table.

Good presenter: Non-verbal signs

1. Recall a good presenter.
2. What did you notice about this person's physiology (his or her face, posture, use of hands, eye contact and movement)?
3. What did you notice about the presenter's vocal delivery (loud, soft, varied, fast/slow pace, volume, pauses, liveliness)?

Physiology	Tonality

What this probably made you realise is that these performance elements made you engage with the content. The presenter's enthusiasm, conveyed in his or her physiology and tone, made you want to listen.

So plan what you will do to improve your performance. What do you need to focus on? It's certainly worth paying attention to your voice. A little voice coaching will help.

Voice coaching

Use the following template to create a speed bio (a vocal biography) of yourself. Take this script and underline key words as in the example below. Actors use these stressed words to tell them when to emphasise a thought or idea. Practise delivering your bio to some friends and ask for feedback. Improve on it and test it out again. Become aware of how you can use your voice.

Voice coaching: Speed bio

1. Look at the example speed biography (bio).
2. Fill in the spaces in your short personal bio.
3. Underline the key words.
4. Practise reading out your bio, emphasising the words you've underlined.
5. Change/amend your bio until you know it reads and sounds really genuine and impressive.

Speed bio – example

I am Meena Mitchell, and I'm the kind of person who is <u>curious</u> about people I meet. I have to <u>stop</u> myself interrogating people sometimes. The <u>most</u> ordinary people have such <u>fascinating</u> stories.

My best success so far was reaching the finals of a poetry competition. It gave me such <u>confidence</u> to know other people would read my poems and <u>enjoy them</u>.

My <u>big</u> life plan is to use poetry in some sort of <u>therapeutic</u> way with kids <u>or adolescents</u>.

Your speed bio

I am _____ and I'm the kind of person who _____

_____

My best success so far has been _____
when _____

My big life plan is to _____

_____

What did you learn from the speed bio exercise?

Best advice for voice delivery Watch or listen to famous speakers like Martin Luther King or Barack Obama. Notice how they use a pause strategically and how they change their pace from slow to fast.

Handling the excitement

It's useful to reframe nervousness as 'excitement'. The two states 'nervous' and 'excitement' are pretty similar, but one word has negative connotations, whereas the other is quite exciting. In fact, those nerves you experience are just a little bit of overexcitement.

So what can you do to ensure that those exciting nerves do not sabotage your performance? Here is the tried and tested best advice.

Tried and tested overexcitement calmers

Preparation – Know the presentation backwards and forwards so that you can virtually do it without notes.

Test-run it a few times to a mirror or a loyal friend, or video yourself.

Drink a glass of water (and sing loudly in the car on the way to the event) to warm up your vocal chords.

Practise cognitive rehearsal,[5] a way of priming your mind for success.

Practise 7/11 breathing[6] every day before the presentation in a relaxed state.

Cognitive rehearsal

This is a technique recommended by psychologists and used by many different performers, including actors and athletes. It is a purposeful visualisation of how you want to 'act' for a given event. Through a purposeful, mental thinking sequence, you are 'rehearsing' a positive experience of delivering a presentation. It is not just wishful thinking. It defuses negative thinking. It allows you to practise being successful hypothetically. By doing this, you set a kind of mind programme for success. It acts to reverse the normal, negative cognitive rehearsal that happens when you find yourself focusing on all the things that can go wrong. You will also be able to use this for interviews or assessment centres to rev yourself up and prime your mind. It will help you present yourself in a most convincing way.

Follow the sequence below. It is best to practise this every day over a week before a presentation or interview.

Cognitive rehearsal practice

Find yourself a quiet place. Sit down. Close your eyes and consciously relax your body.

Notice your breath flowing in and out of your lungs.

Enjoy the relaxed state for a few moments.

Think ahead to the presentation you will give.

See yourself delivering a brilliant presentation.

See how you will look and the impression you will give.

Hear how you will sound. Hear your voice coming out strongly.

Feel how you will feel as you know the presentation is going well.

Imagine it all going perfectly and *see, hear* and *feel* how good that will be.

7/11 breathing

This is a calming breath technique, which works to put you in control of your physical state. It is really simple and effective. Try this now, using the instructions below.

7/11 breathing practice

Find yourself a quiet place.

Close your eyes and consciously relax your body.

Notice your breath flowing in and out of your lungs.

Enjoy the relaxed state for a few moments.

Change your breath pattern. When you breathe in, count to 7.

When you breathe out, count to 11.

Do a few rounds of this breathing pattern.

Notice how you feel.

Chapter 9

Again, this can be practised regularly so that it comes naturally as a de-stressing and calming technique. It can also be used at the beginning of the cognitive rehearsal practice.

Everyday practice for presentations

Take every opportunity to speak out in all kinds of situations. This is the first step to building confidence for presentations. Avoidance of presentations is not going to help you become stronger in this area. There are opportunities through university and part-time jobs to do mini-presentations. You might be a student ambassador or take responsibility for a student society. You could get involved in recruitment days and show prospective students around campus. You might have to train new people at work. These 'presentations' may be informal, and of short duration, but you are toning up and flexing your presentation muscles.

Remember also that presenting yourself to an employer goes way beyond the formal presentation aspect. You will be presenting yourself to the recruiter in every stage of the application process.

Here are some final reminders about presentations.

Summary of key points

Find out as much as you can: Research the employer, and clarify what the company is expecting from the presentation.
Structure what you want to say: Focus this on the topic and the audience.
Practise your performance: Be aware of the non-verbal aspects, and make sure you keep to the time limit.
Be memorable: Find an angle for your presentation which will make you stand out.

Now read the advice from another successful graduate candidate. Notice the positive and resourceful mindset that Cristina demonstrated. This will have permeated her presentation and performance in all the application stages. Graduate job applications for prestigious organisations such as Disney, or even for less well-known companies, will certainly require you to move beyond your personal comfort zone. However, most candidates confirm that this can be the most gratifying part of a successful job campaign. It can be exhilarating to test yourself to the limit.

My Advice – Cristina Garlington,
Employer Branding Communications Coordinator,
Disneyland® Paris

Ask yourself, 'What would I like to accomplish in my career?" and "What would make me happy?' I'd always hoped to perfect my French so when the opportunity came, I grabbed it. My initial contact with Disney, as an employer, was a matter of serendipity following a search on Linkedin. It's great that **social media helps you connect with some very inspiring people** therefore **make sure you continue to develop your network**. It's interesting that many career opportunities aren't published, so do **bear in mind the 'hidden job market'**.

Many of the jobs I've had have materialized by simply speaking to people who've brought my attention to existing offers or potential career paths. A regular application process has then followed. For Disneyland® Paris, I had five interviews before finding a department that felt right.

In the end, **every opportunity is what you make it**. Do your research, be honest about your ability and **never forget your value**. There's nothing better than bringing something new to the table so **make it a win-win!**

I had to **step out of my comfort zone** – learning how to be myself in a different language, which takes time. But I absolutely went for it, and I can now watch films in French without any subtitles!

Surrounding yourself with positive-minded people will help you, and they'll push you far. The most important thing is just to be yourself.

So you now have the know-how to create and deliver a brilliant presentation. This will also help you for the interview section of an assessment centre.

Chapter 9

Find out more

- **Read about the most common fears**
  http://www.psychologytoday.com/blog/brainsnacks/201203/
  the-only-5-fears-we-all-share
- **Change your thinking**
  Altiero, J, 2006, *No More Stinking Thinking*. London: Jessica Kingsley
  Publishers.
- **Learn about communication**
  Bounds, A. 2010. *The Jelly Effect: How to Make Your Communication
  Stick*, Chichester: Capstone Publishing.
- **Set up a Google alert**
  https://www.google.co.uk/alerts
- **Start your LinkedIn profile**
  www.linkedin.com
- **Learn about Prezi**
  https://prezi.com/explore/staff-picks/

What to do next

Take any opportunity you can to deliver a presentation. Test out
some of the ideas and plans from this chapter. Notice your negative
thoughts. Practise cognitive rehearsal.

The interview questions

Contents

Questions are a daily ritual, the most powerful constant in communication. Without questions, verbal communication would grind to a halt. You use and respond to questions every day, without much angst.

Interview questions used within recruitment are not that different. How would you rate how you feel about being asked questions in an interview? Decide where you are on the spectrum of possible viewpoints.

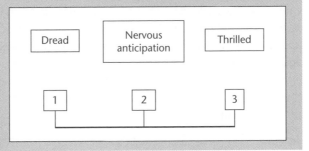

Interview viewpoint spectrum

Mark where you are on the spectrum, according to how you feel about being asked interview questions.

Dread	Nervous anticipation	Thrilled
1	2	3

Many candidates will place themselves in that 'nervous anticipation' point. That's not a bad place to be if it means that you prepare yourself well and can control your nerves. You may be that rarer person yet, who is thrilled by the interview 'cut and thrust'. It still helps to prepare in detail for the interview questions. If it's dread you feel, then you need to have a sure-fire process to protect yourself against this interview foreboding. You need to understand the interview format and the types of questions most often posed. That's the best preparation to dispel fears and change this mind-state. There's more about controlling your mind-state in Chapter 11.

The most common interview format

The format of the interview is the broad structure of the interview from beginning to end. The format chosen by the recruiter acts as a framework for the questions. Here's the most common interview structure:

Introduction: Briefing as to how the interview will be run.

General questions: Why did you apply? What can you offer?

Specific questions: These are related to the job role.

Invitation to interviewee: This is your turn to ask questions.

Ending: The interviewer thanks you and tells you when to expect a decision.

A structured approach

Professional interviewers follow a particular format so that all candidates have broadly the same experience. The aim is to make the process fair and rigorous. The same questions should be asked of each applicant so that interviewers can assess and compare one applicant against another in terms of their responses to the set questions. Each interviewer will decide on a score for each response you give. At the end of the interviews, scores will be used to determine the best-performing applicant.

Scoring

Remember that professional interviewers will score your response to each question on a scale that has been decided by the panel or recruitment professionals.

Other interview arrangements

The one-person or two-person interview panel It is rare these days to be interviewed by just one person, but it still does happen. Ideally, recruiters need to be sure that they gain a fair picture of the candidate. Normally a one-person perception is not deemed sufficient. This might be a pre-selection interview.

The three-person or four-person panel This is more the norm for graduate roles. Panel members will take turns in asking questions derived from the job specification.

Types of interviews

Different recruiters use different types of interview models, according to the recruiter's preference and what he or she wants to find out from applicants. Here's a list of the most common types and what to expect.

Interview types	
Telephone interview	This is often a pre-selection dialogue with a recruiter as part of the shortlisting phase.
Online/video interview (Skype or similar)	This is a virtual interview with a recruiter and may be used for international job roles or as a pre-interview selection procedure.
Biographical interview	Questions revolve around your CV and experience/achievements.
Competency interview	Each question will be related to criteria from the person specification and job description. You will be expected to offer examples to match particular criteria.
Strengths-based interview	Questions are focused around your strengths, skills and qualities.
Behavioural interview	You will be asked to talk through two or three specific events in your career (successes or failures), and probing questions are asked about your personal approach.
Role-play interview	You will be given a scenario and will have to act this out with the interviewer.

These interview types are the most common, so it's worth looking at them in more detail to determine the best way to handle them.

Telephone interview These are typically 15–20 minutes long. Recruiters use them to gain a quick impression of you and your motivation for the job role. They could surprise you with a phone call or book a specific time to phone you.

- Decide where you will take the call. Make sure you will not be disturbed or distracted. Answer the phone professionally with your name and a greeting: 'Hello, it's Claude Allen here.'
- Be very aware of your voice and how it will project. Make sure the words you use match your tonal delivery. It's a good idea to take the call standing rather than sitting. It will allow your lungs to be unconstricted and your voice will sound clearer.
- Speak at a good rate/pace. Remember that as the interviewer cannot see you, he or she will form impressions from your tonal quality. Make sure you sound upbeat and positive.

Online/video interview This is more common as a preliminary to an assessment centre or interview or even for international job roles, often using Skype.[1]

- Check your Internet connection; then register for Skype with a professional name and practise using Skype for a conversation with a friend.
- Find the best environment for the online call. Choose a reasonably light room, and position your laptop/computer or device so that it is level with you. (You do not want to be looking down.)
- Make sure the light is behind the screen.
- Check how you look, and adjust the position of your device until the lighting is good and the angle is flattering.
- Make sure your face and hair look tidy and that you present a professional demeanour (make-up can really help, as camera quality is often not that good).
- Check the sound quality by speaking to your friend.

These kind of virtual interviews are often shorter than an average interview. Most face-to-face interviews are 30 to 60 minutes long typically. Skype interviews are often only 15–20 minutes long and are designed to assess you very quickly. This kind of interview focuses on your motivation to work for that company and your interest in that job role. You will probably be asked about your degree and relevant experience.

Biographical interview This may be an interview with a recruitment agency to determine whether to shortlist you for a job role with a particular employer. It will seem like a 'get-to-know-you' interview but is more testing than that sounds. You will be quizzed about your motivation, your career plan so far and your qualifications, experience and successes. You need to prepare for this by analysing your CV (that will be the agency's starting point) and be ready to be questioned about your personal career goals and drivers.

Competency-based interview (CBI) This is one of the the most common formats for interviews, particularly with big companies. CBIs are used by the NHS and many public sector organisations. They are seen as a fair way to check whether applicants have the competencies laid out in the person specification and job description. These key competencies form the basis for the majority of the interview questions. Each question will be framed around a particular competency, and you will have to give an example of how you match each competency.

The aim of a competency interview is to uncover your skills, talents and abilities relevant to that job role. Read carefully through the job role specification, noting the skills and abilities detailed in the person specification and job description. You need to be ready to offer a convincing example of each competency listed.

Strengths-based interview (SBI) These are quite personal, as the questions are framed to discover your strengths, in terms of skills and qualities, based on what you most like to do, what you choose to do and what your natural talents are. SBIs use positive psychology (Seligman 2003)[2] to determine how you perform, based on your strengths. They can feel so affirming that you might forget you're being interviewed. Questions might include 'When are you happiest?' Make sure you know what you want to 'showcase' about yourself.

Chapter 10

Behavioural interview These can seem confusingly like a competency interview, as the questions often sound similar. You will be asked to talk about your typical behaviour in particular situations and life events. You may be requested to present two or three events in your career so far. These might be negative or positive. The interviewers will ask probing questions designed to reveal your personal approach to risk, your ability to problem-solve, the way you connect with others and your decision-making, as shown in these chosen example events.

The aim is to find out how you would fit within that company or organisation's culture. Make sure that you do intensive research into that employer so that you really know the personality of the company, its mission and purpose. Follow the company on Twitter to get a sense of its personality.

Role-play interview Role plays are a common assessment centre exercise (see Chapter 8). The role-play interview is a variation of this. For medical roles in the NHS, candidates may be given a scenario to act out with the interviewer. The candidate will play the medical professional giving bad news to a patient for example. The interviewer will play the patient.

You will be given the scenario before the interview. You will be given a specified time limit (often about 10 minutes) to 'act' out the scenario. The most important part of a role-play interview is to read this scenario thoroughly. Decide the key issues, and then act it out in the most normal way (as you would for real).

Questions are the lifeblood of interviews and the aspect that causes applicants the most anxiety. It's time to focus on the interview questions.

Types of questions

The interviewers will prepare themselves for the interviews by deciding the best questions to ask, according to the requirements of the job role. Most questions will be directly linked to the job specification.

Analyse the job specification

Professional recruiters use the job role and person specification as the framework for their questions. You need to look at this in-depth. You can predict questions and competencies or strengths they will be seeking. Look at the job advert below. There was no other information. Decide what questions they will probably ask.

Job advert

An online regional business magazine wishes to recruit an editorial assistant to work with the features editor. It will focus on politics, government, thought leadership and business creation. This is a role for someone who

- knows how to create engaging news and features stories;
- is numerate and can deal with complex data;
- is flexible and organised; and
- is social media and web literate.

Have a guess at the questions from the list below.

Guess the possible questions

Decide which questions they will ask, based on the desirable competencies, indicated in the job advert

1. Why are you interested in this job role?
2. What online magazines do you read?
3. What can you offer us specifically?
4. What political issue for businesses is important at the moment?
5. What item of news has sparked your interest in the last week?
6. What does 'thought leadership' mean to you?
7. Give us a feature idea you would like to research and write.
8. Pick your three most influential people in the world of business or politics.

It may be that all these questions are legitimate for this role, but the ones which were used were questions 1, 3, 4, 6, 7 and 8.

What about the term 'thought leadership (Forbes 2013)[3] in the advert? It is a relatively current leadership idea. As it was featured in the advert, it is a hint that this will come up as a question. You need to spot these key words in a job advert. Think of them as buzzwords that indicate something about that employer and what they require from applicants. They are a possible hint of an interview question.

Most candidates do better if they know what to expect. In preparation for the questions, it's useful to consider the most common questions, whatever the format. Begin by thinking about the start of an interview.

Introduction phase

Get ready for an 'icebreaker' question.

Icebreaker questions If you can ace those first moments, it will give you a good momentum for the whole interview. An icebreaker question might be any of the following:

'How did you travel here today?' 'Did you find it easy to park?' 'Have you been to Birmingham before?' 'The weather's been good, hasn't it?'

You get the idea. This is just small talk and designed to settle you down. Smile and greet the interviewers. Respond in a natural and courteous way. Take the opportunity to build a bit of rapport with the interviewer. However, some icebreaker questions are more important than they seem.

Employer's view – Roger Spence, Director, Harrison Drury Solicitors

On an assessment day, the informal part of the process is as important as the formal part.

It gives the candidate an opportunity to shine in a more relaxed way. The informal nature of this 'icebreaker' chat does not mean the candidate is not being assessed. This is considered along with other information we gain from the scenario tasks and the formal interview and CV chat.

General questions

Next, you will have the general or common starter questions.

These will be pretty familiar.

Common general questions
1. Why do you want this job? What interests you about this role? 2. Why do you want to work for (company name)? 3. What do you know about this company/organisation? 4. What can you offer us by way of experience? 5. Tell us about yourself.

Common general starter questions Prepare for these questions to make a powerful beginning. It's useful to create responses based on a simple structure. It makes them easy to remember. Break up your response into three or four chunks. Remember that interviewers will be listening and taking notes. Long rambling answers make it hard for them to pay attention. Try a 'three chunks approach'. Here's how it works. Imagine a youth worker candidate is asked the question 'Why do you want this job?' This is how she might structure her response.

Three chunks approach example	
Why do want this job? (youth work)	
Chunk 1	Firstly, I love working with young people. I find them fascinating and surprising. I want to help them know how much they can achieve.
Chunk 2	Secondly, I have trained for youth work through my degree and through placement experience. I have worked with different young people from different cultures.
Chunk 3	Finally, I love the work of the Prince's Trust and how it inspires and motivates young people from disadvantaged backgrounds to achieve their true potential.

You can prepare three chunks answers for the most common questions. They are memorable because of the chunks and the key words or phrases used.

Chapter 10

Signpost each point you make with 'Firstly, Secondly, Thirdly' or something similar. So in answer to the question

'Why do you want this job?'

You might answer:

'Firstly, this is just the role I want for my first graduate job because my degree study has prepared me perfectly for this kind of nuclear engineering job.

Secondly, placement experience has given me knowledge of hazard recognition which the job requires.

Finally, I like the company culture and the variety suggested by the job role.'

You do not need to learn a full scripted answer. The three chunks structure helps you construct an answer that is clear, convincing and content-rich. Analyse the key buzzwords that you have identified through research into that employer. Make sure that you demonstrate your understanding of that employer and the job role requirements. This kind of 'chunking' allows you to dovetail your answer to the question in a really specific way. It can be used for most questions. Try it out.

General question preparation: Three chunks approach

Question: What can you offer us by way of experience?
1. Think of three examples of your suitability for a job role.
2. Frame them into three chunks.

Chunk 1	_____ _____
Chunk 2	_____ _____
Chunk 3	_____ _____

If you find this difficult at first, do a quick sift through your experience from study, interests, part-time work or volunteering. Look for examples of personal qualities, skills or particular knowledge gained.

Being able to deal with these general starter questions in this way will certainly help you make a good first impression. However this three chunks approach can also be used for other interview questions. Take a look at this social work example.

Social work interview example

Question: How would you deal with a complaint from a service user?

For me it's about *three things*. Firstly, it's about *my relationship with the service user*, how long I have worked with him or her and the nature of the complaint. Secondly, it's about *responding to the complaint, making the service user feel attended to* and dealing with my own feelings. Finally, it's about *personal and professional accountability*. I need to deal with this objectively and fairly, discuss it in supervision and decide on action that is in the *best interests* of the service user.

This should demonstrate that a three chunks approach structures the interview response into neat sections, using short phrases or key words (see italics) that reflect requirements in the job specification.

Specific questions

Competency questions Each competency will be featured in the job specification. You need to come up with a micro-story or convincing example, which proves that you can fulfil that competency. It's worth doing some expansive thinking to come up with these examples. They can be related to work, part-time jobs, placements, some gap year travel you have undertaken or to personal interests or activities.

You will need to create **a memory bank of examples** ready so that you can quickly offer evidence of why you fit the job criteria.

A common competency question is about how you might have dealt with a difficult customer or situation. This is a fairly typical question for job roles, where customer service and teamwork are paramount. It helps to have an answer framework to present this competency.

Try out this adaptation of the *What/So what/Now what* (Driscoll 2000)[4] reflective model structure. It's used by many health professionals to develop their professional practice. Here's how to use it for interview questions.

The What/So what/Now what framework

What – Describe the situation; set the scene.

Give some detail.

So what – So what did you do? What action did you take?

Now what – Say what the result was (ideally successful) and what you learned/realised.

Follow this process to present your competency story in a structured and convincing way. Focus on giving a cast-iron example. Take the 'dealing with a difficult person' scenario as an example. Here's how your answer might look, using this framework.

Competency question: Dealing with a difficult person example

What

I was working in a department store in my summer vacation. It was the sale period, and we were very busy. There were queues at every till. It was really hectic. One customer eventually made it to the front of the queue. She wanted to return something. Returns were dealt with by the Customer Enquiries on the next floor till point.

So what

So, I knew straightaway that she was frustrated and she was holding up the queue and other customers were also irritated. I said to her, 'I'm really sorry you're in the wrong queue for returns. Give me a minute to phone Customer Enquiries so they can expect you. Can I give them your name?' I dialled Customer Enquiries and said, 'There's a really patient customer who needs a fast track Returns process as she has just queued here for over 5 minutes. I am sending her to you, and her name is Mrs Ferren. Please help her!'

Now what

A bit later, the customer passed me and thanked me for my efforts. The thing is, we should have had a sign saying 'No Returns', but overall it could have been worse, and the Customer Enquiries people knew by my tone that I was desperate. For me, staying calm, apologising and taking prompt action was what helped.

You might think that is a long answer, but it is about three paragraphs. That is just about right for a competency question. If you can think through your examples for each competency, you could practise telling your micro-stories. These prove that you are genuinely competent for that competency area of the job specification. These need to be high-quality stories. The examples below are frankly mediocre.

Poor competency question response examples

Give us an example of a time when you have worked in a team to achieve a result.

Well, I worked in a call centre for one year, and we were given team and individual targets each month.

Give us an example of a time when you have worked in a team to achieve a result.

Well, I worked in a call centre for one year, and we were given team and individual targets each month.

Most of the time, I made my targets and helped others when I could.

Chapter 10

The next example is much better. Analyse what attributes are indicated by this candidate's example.

A better competency example

What attributes are demonstrated by this example?

Give us an example of a time when you have worked in a team to achieve a result.

Well, I worked in a call centre for one year, and we were given team and individual targets each month.

You could tell that some people focused on their own targets, but I realised that if we worked together, we could help each other out, as the volume of calls changed all the time.

There were a team of us who regularly sat near to one another. I suggested that we keep our own tally of how many calls we had dealt with and have a competition at the end of each day to push up our stats. We found it was more fun and all of our stats improved.

Another better competency example

What attributes are demonstrated by this example?

Give us an example of a situation you found difficult to handle.

I worked one summer vacation in reception at a sixth form college. One morning, a parent phoned up, asking if his daughter attended the college.

It seemed odd to me that he didn't know this. I realised that it would be wrong to give out any information due to data protection protocols. I explained that I could not do what he asked. He became irate. He threatened to report me to the principal.

I stayed calm and explained that if he wanted to write to the principal, his query would be dealt with. As soon as the phone call ended, I emailed my line manager and copied in the principal, so he was forewarned.

Attributes demonstrated

_____

_____

The attributes that are particularly noticeable in these competency examples are listed here:

- Proactivity
- Commitment
- Motivation
- Leadership
- Teamwork
- Communication.

Here's some good advice from a successful graduate applicant.

My story – Bethany McCrave, Assistant Brand Manager, Unilever

Most of the interview questions I was asked were in the form of 'tell me about a time when you …'. So it's a good idea to have plenty of real-life examples ready to share. It could be from uni or a sports team or volunteer work – no experience is too small as long as you can show you learnt something from it!

Most companies will put some detail about how they assess graduates on their website, so do your research beforehand. Unilever has a set of 'standards of leadership' they look at. Knowing about these made sure I was well prepared for the interviews.

The following competency questions are the most common. They will normally start with 'Tell me about a time when …' or 'Give me an example of …'.

Most common competency questions

Tell me about a time when you had to influence someone else to your point of view.

Tell me about a time when you had to be flexible to deal with a new priority.

Tell me about the toughest challenge you have encountered.

Tell me about a time when you have worked with a difficult group.

Tell me about a time when you exceeded customer expectations (retail).

Tell me about your management style.

Give us an example of when you had to use communication skills to solve a problem.

Give us an example of when you acted in an anti-oppressive way (social work).

Give us an example of a situation you found difficult to handle.

Give us an example of when you showed leadership potential.

Give us an example of when you have analysed data.

Give us an example of when you had to work to a tight deadline.

Remember, you only need to look at the job specification to know the competencies required. It's really easy to predict the competency questions they will ask. Prepare the list of questions you anticipate in a written document or on small cards. Then, construct your structured answers. This is your memory bank of examples. Knowing which example you will offer for each competence will make you feel confident and ready.

Most importantly, you must go beyond just describing the situation in your example of a particular competency. You have to be able to show a positive result for each example (the *So what* aspect). It can be a good idea to show your example answers to a careers adviser or a tutor. They ought to be able to give you feedback on the quality of your examples and how they match the specific competencies.

You can ask someone to role-play the interview with you, using these questions. Fluency in your response is your goal. You want to be able to summon up each example from your memory bank. This can become really natural with a little practice.

Hypothetical scenario questions Sometimes you may be given a verbal or written scenario question to consider and then asked: 'What would you do if ...?' So the interviewer may ask:

'What would you do in a situation if someone took credit for some work you had done?'

These scenarios do not have perfect answers, but you need to show that you can explore the situation in a considered way. Use the QUID structure from Chapter 8 or the *What/So what/Now What* framework.

Strengths-based interview questions (SBI) Some large graduate recruiters have switched to an SBI approach. They believe that SBI interviews work better in identifying potential in candidates. You may find that your interview has both competency and strengths-based questions.

These types of interviews can seem quite personal and even affirming. You are being asked to talk about what you enjoy doing and your talents. If you like talking about yourself, you could relax a bit too much and forget to present the best evidence that will impress the interview panel.

It is still wise to take a structured approach in answering these questions. Avoid a rambling discourse which peters out at the end. Try the **three chunks approach** mentioned earlier. Give the interviewer your three key points or three reasons. So for example, a question such as

'What do you like to do when you have spare time?'

may seem innocuous, so you might be tempted to say,

'Oh, I like playing ice hockey'.

That is a shockingly abrupt answer, so it needs to be expanded to suggest strengths associated with this activity.

Instead you might say:

Three chunks approach: example	
Chunk 1	I love playing ice hockey. I have played since the age of 11, and it's great for fitness, teamwork and coordination.
Chunk 2	Some people think it's a bit too physical but I love the speed and the controlled power you need to play well.
Chunk 3	I think it's helped me be confident and a quick thinker.

Below you can find examples of typical strengths-based questions, but as with competency questions, the interviewers will use questions that are designed to discover and uncover strengths required for that job role. Analyse each question. What is the reason for this question? What do they want to know? There is always an intention or purpose behind the question. Think carefully before answering. Aim to offer something personal and relevant to that work role.

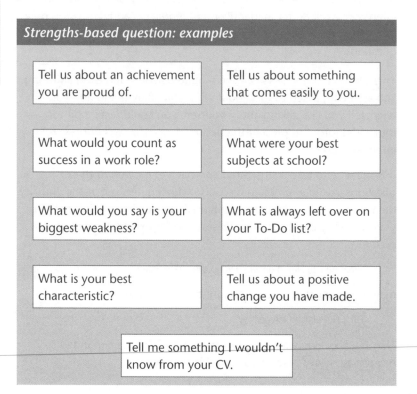

Strengths-based question: examples

Tell us about an achievement you are proud of.

Tell us about something that comes easily to you.

What would you count as success in a work role?

What were your best subjects at school?

What would you say is your biggest weakness?

What is always left over on your To-Do list?

What is your best characteristic?

Tell us about a positive change you have made.

Tell me something I wouldn't know from your CV.

Take a moment to analyse these questions. The answers they generate could be quite revealing. There are underlying themes behind them:

- Achievement
- Success
- Talents
- Self-awareness.

The biggest weakness question can pose a bit of a quandary. Broadly speaking, interview coaches will tell you to avoid giving anything negative about yourself, but this question is almost forcing you to do this. So how can you handle this? The best advice for all strengths-based questions is to be honest. It does not mean you are going to shoot yourself in the foot. It is wise to pick an acceptable weakness to present. Take a look at the following examples, and decide which sounds the best.

Example answers to 'biggest weakness' question

1. 'I'm really hopeless at maths, and if there is anything with numbers in it, I avoid it like the plague.'

2. 'Putting things in writing is not my strong point. If I can talk to someone face-to-face, I prefer it, but I have to remember to follow this up in writing.'

3. 'My friends say I'm terribly grumpy in the morning.'

4. 'I go into the zone sometimes when I have a deadline on a project. I might just work away and not appreciate the others on the project. I have to remind myself that collaborating with others can stimulate creativity and make for a better outcome.'

5. 'I eat too much chocolate and drink too much coffee. It makes me hyper.'

6. 'I avoid office communication meetings as they tend to overrun. It means that I am sometimes out of the loop and a bit behind the curve about what's going on. I've got to find a way to keep up to speed and so have suggested an intranet office communication space.'

You'll probably notice that answer 4 is the best. It is honest and yet shows self-awareness. Answers 2 and 5 are a little too revealing. Answers 1 and 6 suggest a negative mindset.

Make sure that you bear in mind the intention of the SBI question. An SBI question is designed to make you reveal something about yourself. Select your answer with this in mind, and disclose something positive and authentically impressive about yourself.

Behavioural interview questions You need to prepare examples of how you have displayed particular commendable behaviours, as suggested by the job role profile. Notice the personal qualities listed. How can you offer evidence that you would behave in a way that would 'show off' the personal qualities which that employer requires? You will have prepared a bank of examples of your skills and abilities for a competency interview. Now add to this with examples of your behaviour in remembered situations. Make sure that these examples demonstrate particular personal attributes, indicated by the job role profile.

Here's an example of what one major recruiter looks for in their graduates. (Nuclear Graduates scheme 2015).[5] Notice the personal attributes they are asking for:

- Flexibility
- Passion
- Commitment
- Initiative
- Independence.

Using the *What, So what, Now what* framework, you can create a 'story' about each of these attributes. Choose a situation (*what*) from your experience (from your studies, from work, interests or travel) that indicates the particular behaviour or attitude which the recruiter requires (*so what* you did), and finish with a positive result ideally (*now what*).

Here's an example:

Flexibility/Initiative – One graduate worked as a volunteer at a university open day for prospective students. On the morning of the event, there was an unexpected train strike. There was a concern that this might put off visitors. She suggested that they put out some quick Facebook and Twitter posts with links to replacement bus services and motorway directions. Her behaviour in this situation proved she possessed the required qualities.

The personal attributes required by the Nuclear Graduates scheme are common to many graduate employers. Think about your evidence for these attributes, and create an additional bank of examples.

Ethical, and equality and diversity questions Dependent on the job role and organisation, there will be specific questions particular to the organisational culture and to the mission and vision they espouse. The NHS and many public sector organisations will generally have an equality and diversity question such as 'What does equality and diversity mean to you?' Notice the buzzwords that come up on company websites and in published articles about particular small or large organisations. Check that you understand these terms and can explain this understanding, if required. If you have researched them well, you will understand what these terms mean to them. You can then prepare your answers. Check their websites, and you will find all you need to know, including their mission/vision type statements.

Quirky questions Below you will find a list of 'quirky' questions. They are unusual and sometimes surprising. You may not be able to prepare for them, as they change all the time, but you can be forewarned about them. Try to deal with them in a positive, resourceful way.

Quirky question examples	
Personal	**Mad and impossible**
What comic book hero would you be and why?	How many sugar cubes would fit into a minicar?
Who would play you in the film of your life?	Do you believe in conspiracy theories?
If we rang three people who worked with you, what would they say about you?	Name one person who you think deserves a Nobel prize.

The 'How many sugar cubes' question is just a way of testing your critical reasoning at work. You will have to go for a reasoned guess. You need to show how you reason this out, whichever answer you come up with. You might start with guessing rough dimensions of the car and guessing a sugar cube to be one cubic centimetre. It's not about the maths. It's about how you would go about it.

Chapter 10

SWERVE Tactics There may be some mad question that you cannot anticipate. It is best to think of a broad approach to these mostly unexpected and often, unanswerable questions. They sometimes reveal reserves of creativity and sheer boldness in candidates. A plan is useful in handling the unexpected.

The mnemonic SWERVE is a useful sequence for avoiding the traps of these types of questions. This is how it works. As with other mnemonics, you follow the sequence of the letters as a prompt for your thinking. It will help you offer a good explanatory answer.

SWERVE sequence	
S	*Situation/scenario* – restate it
W	*What* (define the problem)
E	*Explain* thinking
R	*Reasons*
V	*Value* of your suggestion
E	*End* with decision

Here's a SWERVE worked example.

SWERVE worked example	
Question: Name someone who deserves a Nobel prize	
S	*Situation/scenario* – 'So I need to think of someone deserving ...'.
W	*What* – 'The problem is, is to define "deserving".'
E	*Explain* thinking – 'I like the idea of nominating someone less well known, like the woman who is bringing kids together in Palestine at the moment. She is fighting the odds and getting children to play together regardless of race and religion.'
R	*Reasons* – 'There are lots of deserving people who are less known. but this charity has helped hundreds of kids.'
V	*Value* of my suggestion – 'She would be a good nomination because the publicity would attract donations, and her life has been consumed by this work. A trip to Norway would be great for her.'
E	*End* with decision – 'Yes – she would be my nomination.'

Invitation to the interviewee

It's usual at one point in the interview, normally close to the end, for one interviewer to ask you 'Do you have any questions for us?' This can throw some applicants if they are not prepared for this. Think about what questions you could ask of a recruiter that would be counted as 'good' questions.

Take a look at the example questions in the box below. What would you count as a good question?

Possible questions	Good/bad
1. Why do you like working for this company/ organisation?	
2. When will my salary increase?	
3. What further training will I need to undertake for this role?	
4. How will recent government budget plans impact on the business?	
5. What plans do you have to expand into ...?	
6. How many weeks, holiday will I get each year?	
7. When will I hear the outcome of this interview?	
8. What do you hope I will achieve in this role?	

Remember that you want to come across as someone who has researched the organisation. Avoid asking obvious questions, especially when this information has been provided on the website. Questions 3, 7 and 8 are positive and presuppose you might be offered the job. They suggest your enthusiasm and hopeful expectations of the role. Questions 4 and 5 suggest that you are interested in that employer's success and the challenge which that company faces. Questions 2 and 6 seem a little too self-interested and may put an employer off. Question 1 is an interesting question but might discomfort an interviewer.

Ending

Often candidates' energy levels flag as they come close to the end of an interview. You need to actively retain a confident posture and confident responses throughout the interview. Perhaps you can save some really excellent example for the last section of the interview to make yourself memorable. It is particularly important to avoid looking like you are glad it's over. Leave the room with your head held high, smiling and thanking the interviewers. If you're feeling confident, you could try the 'Oh, and One Last Thing' tactic.

Oliver used this in his interview for a large cinema group. Here's what he said.

My story – Oliver Cotton, Assistant Manager, Odeon Cinema

I was asked if I had any questions. I said, 'No, you've covered everything. By the way … I wanted to mention that the Film Society season you're running has a great line-up. Cameron Crowe's film *Almost Famous* is one of my favourite films. I'm in a rock band, and I think you could put on a themed season featuring rock bands. You could start with the Beatles in *Hard Day's Night*, then go for *This is Spinal Tap* or *Gimme Shelter* or the Dylan documentary *Don't Look Back.* I think it would bring the rock crowd in. That's something I'd love to organise. I think it worked to make me stand out from the other applicants.

Can you see how that might give a strong and enthusiastic finish to the interview? Just be aware that you need to give yourself a strong start *and* finish to offer a completely compelling interview performance. Finally, take a look at the key success factors for a brilliant interview performance.

Success factors for interviews

The first impression

A strong start is part of the 'first impression' segment. Research into impression management (Goffman 1959)[6] and self-presentation (Leary 1996)[7] confirms that impressions are formed at lightning speed. You make up your mind fast about a stranger. The evolutionary imperative to survive meant that human beings needed to tell the difference between friend and foe. (You can find more about this in Chapter 11.)

> 'We form a sense of whether a stranger is trustworthy in less than a tenth of a second.' (BPS Digest 2014)[8]

Recruiters are just like you and form similar rapid impressions about applicants in the beginning moments of an interview. Be aware of this 'first impression' tendency, and make it work for you. You can build rapport by offering a handshake, pitching your voice at the same level as the interviewer's (the same volume level) and responding politely and warmly to the icebreaker questions.

Self-awareness – the magic ingredient

Any interview is ultimately a test of your self-awareness, a constant theme in this book. Interviewers expect you to be able to talk about yourself and your strengths. Your degree subject may have been valuable, but your degree of self-knowledge will be just as important. Read Emily's story to see why.

My story – Emily C graduate

I haven't had many interviews … but they always ask me the same questions. They always ask me to tell them a situation where I had to deal with a difficult customer and a situation where I had to deal with a difficult staff member.

Another one was I had to give three words that a friend would use to describe me.

One part of Emily's experience was a typical competency-based question. It's that difficult customer/situation scenario again. However, the 'three words question' is also a useful exercise. It is asking you to think of your personal attributes. If you stumble over that, you seem a bit unprepared and vague. Think about it.

> Give three words that a friend would use to describe you.

How easy is it to come up with those three words? It's worth thinking about this. Ask friends and family for ideas. You could even use a thesaurus to find words that you feel most accurately express who you are. Think of yourself as a project. This is a small but important research activity which will help you see yourself as others see you. You need to know yourself and your personal qualities. Knowing how you come across to others will help you recognise the qualities you have. It will mean that you are confident to present yourself in a genuine way. You can also go back to Chapter 2 and revisit the self-assessment activity. Reassess your findings for further clues to help you acknowledge your own personal strengths.

So whatever you discover, aim to focus on the positives. Notice the repeated words or themes from what people say about you. It's useful to select the words that relate to particular work attributes. The following self-knowledge quiz might help you be aware of the kind of attributes recruiters require (that link to your personal qualities). You may pick other words to describe yourself, but these are a good start.

Self-knowledge quiz: Assess yourself

1. Decide if you have each attribute listed, and tick it if you do.
2. Think of an example that would prove you possess that attribute.

	Attribute	Tick	Example of this attribute
1	Organised		
2	Persuasive		
3	Motivated		
4	Flexible		
5	Committed		
6	Passionate		
7	Innovative		
8	Proactive		

That's a good start on your interview preparation in terms of the questions. Here's a summary of the perfect interview preparation.

Summary – Key success factors

Research the employer: Go beyond a simple website search. Do an online news trawl for recent articles about the company. Track it on social media. Find out about its interview methods.

Second-guess questions: You need to prepare for the standard questions by analysis of the job specification. Know the key words and phrases you want to use to convey who you are and why you are the best applicant.

Be aware of first impressions at interview: Aim to present yourself in a convincing way and build rapport with your interviewers.

Be authentic and show self-awareness: You need to be yourself on your best form. Knowing yourself and what you can offer is the basis for authentic responses to interview questions.

To finish, read some good advice from a recruiter.

Chapter 10

Employer's view – Luke Frost, Talent Manager, BBC Children's TV

Research

If I only had a pound for every time I have interviewed someone desperate to work in Children's TV, but who could not name a single programme we make. There is no excuse for it. Research is key.

Examples

You should be able to back up all your answers with plenty of examples. This lets you demonstrate your experience and tells us how you would handle a situation. Don't worry if the outcome was not what you hoped for. Just explain why it went wrong and what you would do differently. But make sure your example relates to the question.

Pause for breath

Don't be afraid of the silence. After the question has been asked, take a minute to gather your thoughts.

Know your audience

Your interview invite should always tell you who your interview panel are. Try to research them if possible, but at the very least be clear about what they do.

What to wear

Working out what to wear can be tricky. First impressions count so dress to impress. Suits aren't necessary but dressing smartly shows you are a professional and keen to impress.

Find out more

- **Competency-based interviews**
  http://www.jobs.ac.uk/careers-advice/interview-tips/1552/how-to-be-more-than-competent-in-competency-based-interviews/
  Read about how to be more than competent in competency-based interviews.
- **Strengths-based interviews**
  https://targetjobs.co.uk/careers-advice/interview-types/275395-strengths-based-interviews-for-jobs-and-grad-schemes
- **Positive psychology**
  https://www.authentichappiness.sas.upenn.edu/
  Learn about changing your mindset.

What to do next

Create your memory bank of examples of the common competencies recruiters require. Write these micro-stories from your own experience. Keep these ready in a document. Practise explaining these examples out loud to a friend. Become comfortable with your chosen competence examples.

Interview preparation

Contents

Think back to your first day at university. For most students, it involves a bombardment of new experiences and quickly established friendships.

The 'first impressions' effect (Goffman 1990)[1] is a big part of these early social interactions. It's probable that you made some instant decisions and bonded with some people quickly. It turns out that these instant decisions are based on numerous tiny, non-verbal signals picked up from one another. More than often, these first impression decisions are surprisingly correct in terms of picking new friends:

> 'First impressions of others can be remarkably accurate' (APA 2005).[2]

Recruitment interview situations provide a particular example of the power of these first impressions. There is a 'thin slice', 30 seconds of time (Ambady and Rosenthal 1992)[3] at the beginning of any interaction, when a powerful, formative impression is conveyed. As a candidate, you need to know how to use this 'first impression advantage' at the beginning of an interview.

The first impression advantage

You need to consider the way you present yourself in the first moments of an interview and work out what creates a positive or negative impression. This is made up of several aspects:

- Your choice of clothing and general appearance (see 'What to wear').
- Your handshake (if there is the chance to shake hands).
- Your eye contact.
- Your posture from the minute you walk through the door.
- The tone, volume and pace of your voice.

Handshake Think of the handshake as a powerful social courtesy, and a rapport builder. It shows that you are aware of the conventions of professional behaviour. Focus on offering a handshake that is firm and confident. Research suggests that a good handshake gives an impression predominantly of 'conscientiousness' (Bernieri and Petty 2011)[4], a most desirable quality from a recruiter's point of view.

Eye contact This is the most regularly noticed body language signal. Lack of eye contact is generally perceived as lack of confidence or general nervousness. Gentle and regular eye contact in a conversation or interview is generally recommended. This signifies interest and a willingness to relate to another human being. Over and above this general benefit, there is evidence that positive eye contact is interpreted as a sign of intelligence (Jarrett 2014)[5].

When there are two, three or four faces on the panel, it is tricky to know where to look. Aim to keep the whole panel in your peripheral eye view (move your chair back a little to see them all better), and give more focused eye contact to each person as he or she asks a question.

Posture Think about this. In simple terms, when you are happy and relaxed, your posture is alert, balanced, open and assured. When you are tense, your shoulders hunch, and your physical presence is somehow diminished. Your postural presence creates an initial positive or negative perception in the interviewer's mind, which can be hard to dispel (Rowh 2012)[6].

Actively regulate your posture by standing tall, relaxing your shoulders and opening out your chest. This will mean that your posture indicates optimal readiness for the interview conversation. It will also help with your voice projection, as your lungs will be unrestricted. Remember to retain this alert but relaxed posture throughout the interview, even when you are seated.

Tone of voice Nervousness can often make your voice come out in a croak. Tense vocal chords affect your voice projection, as does panicky breathing. You need to pitch your voice at the right level, injecting warmth and animation into your delivery.

The power of your 'Hello' is not to be overlooked.

> 'Psychologists from universities of Glasgow, Scotland, and Princeton, US, have shown that a simple "Hello" is enough to allow most people to draw conclusions about personality type' (McAleer).[7]

In addition, the right kind of tonality has been found to signify trustworthiness (McAleer)[8], another quality which employers value. For more on voice practice, remember and/or revisit what was covered in Chapter 9.

So it would seem that these first impression ingredients could really be extraordinarily important in getting your interview off to a convincing start. Imagine this. In the first few seconds, you could give an impression of intelligence (eye contact), conscientiousness (handshake) and trustworthiness (tonality). Not a bad start at all! It's time to consider other aspects of the interview dynamic.

The interview dynamic

The interview dynamic is something over and above the asking and answering of questions. This dynamic is a two-way, non-verbal interplay between what is going on in your head and that of the interviewer. Professional interviewers will be aware of the subjective nature of first impressions. They will try to be rigorous in being objective in their assessment of you. However, interviewers are human beings, and they pick up and interpret micro-impressions, from your face particularly. These can be hard to disregard if they are off-putting.

Your interview impression is made up broadly of these two components:

- The verbal dynamic – how you respond to the questions and what those answers reveal about you and your suitability for the job role (Chapter 10).
- Non-verbal dynamic – how you seem, how your physiology (body language) is interpreted.

It's really useful to continue by analysing your own non-verbal, self-presentation.

The non-verbal dynamic

Interview nervousness is common. This nervous state produces confusing 'tells' (Collett 2004)[9], the common body language signs that obscure and cloak the real you. These can result in misperceptions by interviewers and assessors, based on your non-verbal performance. You need to find a way to control these 'tells' so that you do not send out confusing signals.

Thoughtless thinking

That brain of yours processes about 70 000 thoughts a day.[10] How many do you recall? It's not easy. Some thoughts barely register. They are those 'thoughtless thoughts', often a stream of subconscious mutterings. They come and go with barely a memory trace. However, these thoughts trigger 'tells' on your face and physiology which may be picked up, often subconsciously, by an interviewer. It may be that your thoughts are 'good' thoughts such as 'I am so ready for this interview', 'I really want to work here' or similar. Conversely, you may be thinking grim thoughts such as 'This is going to wrong' or 'I will mess up'.

This negative brain activity can take over, so you need to be aware of it and control it throughout the interview. Being aware of your own mind-state and directing your own thoughts, is one way to create the most powerful impression.

Take a look at Nafisa Sayani's story.

My story – Nafisa Sayani, Broadcast Journalist, BBC South East Today

My best job interview experience was one for which I had prepared thoroughly and as a result was armed with confidence to sell myself. I had prepared as much as I could. The assessment wasn't easy, with two written exams and a panel interview. When they asked me a question I didn't know the answer to, it would have been easy to let the nerves overpower me. But instead of letting it fluster me, I elaborated on what I did know and made it clear I was enthusiastic and keen to find out more. The next day I received a phone call – I had got the job.

Nafisa was able to control her nerves through preparation and control of her thinking. She did not let the nerves get in the way of a genuine and enthusiastic performance.

Mind-state work

The goal is to be able to present yourself accurately and authentically as someone who is capable of taking on a particular job role. This is a mental preparation, your mind-state work. There are three key stages to this:

Accurate self-presentation

Train your mind	Know what to show	Know the employer

Train your mind

The best way to control your 'tells' (those body language signs), your nerves and your actual performance is by doing some work on your mind-state (the inside of your head). Realise this. What you think on the inside of your head, good or bad, might 'leak' out in your non-verbal or body language. It's related to cognitive rehearsal (Chapter 9). Your thoughts, positive or negative, affect your posture, your tone of voice and your general demeanour.

Chapter 11

Be aware of the disabling power of negative thoughts Often when something goes wrong in an interview, it is because the candidate has rehearsed a negatively projected scenario in his or her mind over and over again. It's a kind of craziness, but some applicants actually practise being terrible 'mentally' by allowing thoughts of bungled questions to take hold of their minds.

Use positive visualisations instead Why not practise being brilliant 'mentally' instead? Fix a picture in your mind of how well the interview could go. Rehearse a positive performance mentally. Practise this through visualisation or cognitive rehearsal (see Chapter 9 and Chapter 12 for more about this). This strong 'thought picture' will create external positive 'tells'. What you are thinking on the inside sets a negative or positive vibe in your body language. This is observable to interviewers.

Take a look at the diagram below. If you can actually visualise you are going to do well, this positive internal imagining will impact on the external 'tells', displayed in your body language (physiological signs). You will seem more confident because you are controlling your thoughts.

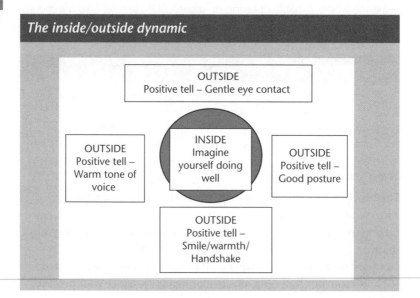

The inside/outside dynamic

OUTSIDE
Positive tell – Gentle eye contact

OUTSIDE
Positive tell –
Warm tone of
voice

INSIDE
Imagine
yourself doing
well

OUTSIDE
Positive tell –
Good posture

OUTSIDE
Positive tell –
Smile/warmth/
Handshake

Know what to show

Most employers will have provided one or all of the following:

- A person specification (their ideal person formula).
- A job role specification (the exact requirements of the job) or job advert.

Take this collection of job role data and analyse it line by line. Decide how and why you match each and every aspect. You are aiming to 'show' a 90% match, ideally. Think of a real example for why you match each aspect, and note this down. Here's an example of how an applicant offered evidence of a match to the company's ideal criteria.

Job role matching example	
Ideal criteria	**Applicant evidence**
Motivation to work in the construction sector	I have worked part-time for a small building firm throughout university and have recently completed a project on contract compliance.
Leadership experience	I have undertaken an ILM leadership award and was team leader for a knowledge transfer project with a local architect's practice.
Achievement-oriented	I set myself goals for work in construction and gained a range of experience through part-time, vacation and sandwich placement work.
Well-developed judgement and integrity	A recent project required me to consider and assess competing bids for a contract. I had to assess a range of factors including sustainability, community benefit and financial costings. I achieved a mark of 65% and believe this demonstrates my critical thinking and professional approach.

This applicant has offered really good examples of why she is suited to this job role. She has demonstrated that she knows her own potential and that she understands what the employer wants. You will need to show this kind of self-awareness in job applications so that you make the shortlist. Following that, you will need to do the same in the interview.

Proof of your capability Create genuine examples in this way as proof that you know yourself and what you can offer an employer. This is the best kind of interview preparation.

Being able to clearly express in words exactly how you match each of the criteria is a good written exercise and will prepare you for the potential questions you will be asked in an interview. That dynamic relationship between you and the interviewer is forged by your willingness to focus on what the employer has explicitly stated in their requirements.

Try a mapping exercise The next exercise encourages you to show this kind of self-awareness by mapping your own evidence examples against a chosen career sector or job role. The criteria listed are common to many graduate roles.

Think of examples from your own experience which would convince an employer of your suitability. This is a valuable prompt for your self-awareness.

Self-awareness: Knowing what to show

Note down in the sections below an example of each of the criteria required by an employer (related to your career preference).

Employer criteria	Your evidence
Motivation to work in your chosen career sector	
Leadership experience	
Achievement-oriented	
Well-developed judgement and integrity	

Career motivation Try to think of strong reasons for choosing that career sector. These reasons will be focused on:

- a genuine interest in that job role; and
- your confidence that you possess the right mix of skills, abilities and experience to perform well in that career.

Most of all, aim to show enthusiasm for that career sector.

Leadership experience You need to show your leadership potential through any examples you can recall of when you have taken responsibility and shown leadership. Obvious examples may be through team sports, but being a student representative for your course, being treasurer for a university society, Duke of Edinburgh–type activities or part-time job experience may offer good examples.

Achievement-oriented This may be related to leadership experience. You will need to recall small or large successes in your study, work, sport or travel experiences. It helps if you have a competitive nature. You don't have to save a rainforest, but you do need to think expansively about your life. Even small achievements can suggest this type of achievement-focused attitude.

Well-developed judgement and integrity Think of a time when you had to weigh up a situation before making a judgement. You might have had to resist the temptation of a night out before an important exam. You might have had to give some honest feedback to a team member in a study project. These types of minor life events can offer strong examples of your ability to make considered judgements and display integrity.

Know the employer

Recruiters are not expecting you to be smarmy, but they are self-interested enough to expect you to have checked them out in depth. A cursory glance at their web page won't be enough, so take some time to investigate the employer.

Here's a reminder of research approaches covered in Chapter 9.

Social media spaces Start with the company website but check its LinkedIn company page/Facebook page. Follow its Twitter feed. Make yourself known to the company through insightful tweets.

Check the business directories in a university library; these are now online for the most part.

Best companies lists See if the company features in any of the 'best' companies lists. Try the Forbes list, Glassdoor and the Sunday Times 100 Best Companies lists (see Chapter 1).

Chapter 11

Online newspaper search Use the company name as a key word, and trawl through recent articles featuring it.

Set up a Google alert for anything about the company.

Mostly, try and find something surprising or really current about the company. You can then use this as a reason for wanting to work for this organisation. This will help you with that perennial interview question: 'Why do you want to work for us?' Be ready for this, and try to avoid a clichéd answer.

What interviewers want

Be authentic

Interviewers complain that many candidates come across as a bit fake or artificial, and this may be due to the unnatural set-up of job interviews. It is your mission to remain authentically you – you on your best day – in what is a weird situation. So whilst it is a formal situation, aim to:

- Retain a relaxed alertness that allows the real you to shine out.
- Smile and ask for questions to be repeated if necessary.
- Build rapport with the panel or single interviewer by treating it like a conversation with a purpose rather than an oppressive cross-examination.

Read what Christine Mabilat from Disney recommends.

Employer's view – Christine Mabilat,

Director of Employer Brand, Talent Acquisition & Total Rewards at Disneyland® Paris

The Interview – Be proud, be curious, be yourself! We want to meet the person you've written about on your CV. If you say you speak three European languages fluently, that's fantastic. Just ensure you can truly speak them, because we usually conduct language tests during the interview. Disneyland® Paris is the largest single-site employer in France, with more nationalities amongst its workforce than any other country in Europe (100 nationalities in total). This is to accommodate our Guests, who come from all over Europe, in their native language. Languages are therefore key for the majority of our roles.

If our recruiter asks to see examples of your work, use this as an opportunity to show us what you can do. We want to hear about your talents and background! It's also essential to do your research beforehand and have an idea of what you're looking for; ask questions and make sure you use the time of your interview wisely.

The Company, Its Product and Culture From a professional standpoint, it helps to like the product at a company you're applying to; at Disneyland® Paris, for example, being a Disney fan is great, but not enough to get you the job – you need to demonstrate your skills and motivation when applying for that specific role. Be honest with yourself: do you have what it takes and will this job make you happy?

Make them pick you

Mostly, imagine that your job is to help them pick you by giving them plenty of reasons to be certain that you fit the role specification.

Imagine being an interviewer who might be seeing six to eight candidates a day over three days. Take a moment to decide what would make someone memorable. Obviously, interviewers take notes, scoring candidates against the job specification, but what would make a particular applicant stand out?

What interviewers notice

Here's what interviewers say they notice. Call them the standout qualities.

The standout qualities list

Make yourself stand out at an interview.
1. Warmth/friendliness
2. Good examples/micro stories from experience
3. Clear explanations – lack of rambling
4. Varied pace of delivery – prosody
5. Enthusiasm for the role

> 6. Resilience
> 7. Confidence to ask for clarification
> 8. Occasional surprising but commendable response
> 9. Smooth entrance and exit
> 10. Confident farewell and thanks to interviewers

Most of these are self-explanatory. Numbers 1 and 5 are about coming across as a living, breathing human being, not a robot. Social courtesies like smiles and handshakes go a long way. In addition, you can show enthusiasm through small words and phrases such as 'I love to ...' and 'I really like to ...'.

Number 2 on the list gives you permission to offer real examples to back up your response to a question. So you might say, 'I had to deal with difficult customers in my work at a call centre. An example of this is when ...'. These are short, micro stories that really make you come across authentically. Make sure you have these stories/examples ready to share (remember this from Chapter 10).

Number 4 is about breathing between sentences and letting enthusiasm into your voice through the words you use and variation in tone. Allow your voice to go up and down (prosody) to avoid a monotone delivery.

Number 6 is a reminder to be resilient. There may be a question which throws you a little or that you even mess up. Just pick yourself up and bounce back with the next one.

Number 7 is a reminder to check that you have understood what is being asked.

Number 8 is about trying to avoid clichés and making your stories a little different from the obvious. You want to surprise the interviewer in a good way.

Numbers 9 and 10 are about making a good ending. Don't rush out as if you are escaping. Ask questions yourself, and make a cool exit.

What to wear

One of the most common concerns from interview applicants is the choice of what to wear. How would you decide the most appropriate clothes choice for your interview?

There are so many different companies and work sectors, and each has its own culture and related work dress rules. Try this quick exercise. On any train or bus journey, take a look at the passengers. Notice those who seem to be on the way to work. Guess their employer. You'll see some passengers who are wearing formal suits. Others may have gone for a smart casual look. Some may be extremely casual. A PE teacher or gym employee may be in track pants and T-shirt. Take a look at the following job roles, and guess the dress code for that career sector.

What to wear: Guess the dress codes	
Journalist	Fashion buyer
_____	_____
_____	_____
Social worker	Landscape architect
_____	_____
_____	_____
PR account manager	Biomedical scientist
_____	_____
_____	_____
Management consultant	Site manager
_____	_____
_____	_____

There are two key questions to ask in determining the dress code for a particular job:

1. Who does this person meet in the job role?
2. Where does this person work?

Journalists may be office-based or out and about on the streets, visiting ordinary people in their houses. They will dress in a smart but informal way which shows respect for those they interview, without being too official or dressed up.

Fashion buyers, whilst mostly office-based, will travel and meet suppliers. There will be an expectation that they dress in a way that shows they know fashion trends and can put an outfit together creatively with accessories.

Social workers may be office-based or visiting clients. Like the journalist, they will not want to seem over-dressed or formal.

Landscape architects and **construction site managers** will work in inside and outside locations. They will be expected to wear appropriate safety equipment and warm, serviceable clothes.

PR account managers deal with corporate clients and will generally wear very smart suits that conform to business dress expectations.

Management consultants will do the same.

Scientists, who often work in laboratories, may wear lab coats some of the time, so a smart but informal look is usual.

The interview dress code

As a general rule, take account of the usual everyday dress code for that job role. However, most applicants go for a slightly more formal interview dress than everyday apparel.

Whilst dress codes may seem flexible once you are in a job, it is still usual to wear an extremely smart, 'suited and booted' look for interviews with the more traditional employers. Remember that research suggests that smart dress sense is equated with success:

> 'Dressing smartly communicates success.' (Jarrett 2014)[11]

Even for those where a smart casual look might be the norm, it is generally safer to dress up rather than down for the interview.

The consensus view

Dress for the sector you are applying for. City finance jobs require a more formal suited look. Youth workers will go for a smart casual look.

Summary of best dress advice

A smart look: Aim for a smart, tailored look which is comfortable and suits your shape.

Travelling: Think of how much you will need to walk, how far you will travel, the time of year and what you will be carrying.

> **Handshake:** A slim bag or briefcase is better so that you are free to shake hands.
>
> **Light colour at neck:** Try a light colour, such as white or cream, for a shirt or blouse, as such colours act to light up the face.
>
> **Fitted shape:** Fitted jackets and trousers/skirts give you a professional look.
>
> **Ties and jewellery:** Avoid loud ties and jangly jewellery as these distract the interviewers.
>
> **Think top to toe:** Get a good haircut and make sure you have smart, polished shoes.
>
> **Check dress code:** Match your choice to the type of employer.

Finally, take some time to think about the whole interview performance, taking account of the non-verbal dynamic, the actual preparation you do and how you present this as a perfect package.

Performing to potential

Knowing what you have to offer (your potential) is one aspect of interview performance. Self-analysis and self-awareness will help you to prepare for the assessment centre and the interactional challenge of an interview. However, knowing yourself and presenting yourself are two separate aspects of this. These two aspects are entwined in a 'potential plus performance' package.

Think of the word potential. It can mean either of these:

● Your actual capability.
● Your likely capability.

In real terms, an interview is designed to uncover your actual potential and your future, perhaps untapped potential. This potential is measured by your performance in the interview or a presentation or in some assessment centre exercise.

Performance is potential

Unfortunately, your performance *is* your potential as far as interviewers can tell. That's all they get. They have to make their judgement based on the fragments of data they gain from your performance.

This 'performance' word summons up visions of a circus seal balancing a ball. It has a connotation of 'acting'. It suggests pretence. However, 'performance' can also mean 'doing', 'being' and 'working'. If your computer performs its functions, it's not an 'act'. It's just being a computer. So your 'performance' is just your 'doing' and 'being' mode.

You will need to perform so that you present yourself authentically as a worthy candidate. That means that you cannot let anything interfere with your natural performance.

You will perform to your potential if you can control any tendency you have to get in your own way. Call it self-sabotage when you allow negative thoughts to destabilise your confidence. Eliminate the self-sabotage, and you will be performing to potential.

Staying resilient

It can be a gut-wrenching business applying for jobs, being rejected and keeping going despite setbacks. It may take more time and effort than you think to achieve success in the graduate job market. It's worth realising that the typical time delay from application to job offer is about 13 weeks (CIPD 2015)[12]. This is very much the norm, so you will need to be persistent and retain an optimistically resilient spirit. You need to manage your own mind-state and self-talk to keep yourself going and to help you bounce back from the odd interview that goes wrong.

It is always worth asking for feedback from interviews or assessment centres. This is often offered as a 'debrief' by larger companies, on request. But mostly, you need to review your performance (acknowledging what went well) and determine what went wrong to avoid this in the future. The following advice comes from a graduate who toughed it out in the construction sector downturn.

Chapter 11

Employer's view – David Isichei, Construction Site Manager, Balfour Beatty

You must always keep faith in your abilities. If you have a knock-back, it's important to show your next potential employer that you are able and keen to succeed.

Get in training

Seeing yourself as others see you

It is worth enlisting the help of a friend or careers adviser to practise being 'interrogated'. Request feedback from your 'interrogator' on your body language, your tonal delivery and overall demeanour. Even in well-delivered interviews, there is this feeling of being interrogated. The next exercise is designed to help you to get used to the 'interrogation dynamic' and 'showcase' yourself in an authentic way.

The aim of this quick-fire interrogation is to force you to talk about yourself. It will also speed up your thinking. You may find you stumble or repeat yourself. With practice, it will become easier. So run through this activity a few times to build awareness of yourself and to become fluent at expressing yourself. Remember to ask for feedback on your body language and voice projection.

Speed interrogation: Twenty questions

Ask a friend to fire these questions at you.

What did you want to be when you were little?
What were you like at primary school?
Give me your three best talents.
Tell me of a key event in your life so far.
What is your perfect day?
What do you look for in a friend?
What makes you smile?
What's your coping strategy for when something goes wrong?
Why did you pick your degree subject?
What do you want from your career?
Who do you admire?
What's important to you in life?
What's your favourite music?
What is your favourite film?
What is your favourite food?
What really makes you mad?
What was the best module or course in your degree?
What are your three best skills?
What subjects did you do best in at school?
What did you enjoy most at school apart from the lessons?

So how did you do? You might have loved talking about yourself. Equally, you might have got off to a slow start. This is a really valuable way to improve fluency in your responses.

Here's some last thoughts from Maya Dibley, another successful graduate.

Employer's view – Maya Dibley, Associate Publisher, Hearst Magazines, UK

There is no one set of tricks that will help you ace an interview, because every interviewer is an individual with his or her own preferences of the type of person he or she wants to work with.... You should always be professional.... You have to be interested in news and developments (for that industry) ... The more you can do that, the more at ease and relaxed you'll be when a question you haven't prepared for comes up in an interview.

Find out more

- Laboratory of Neuro Imaging (LONI)
  www.loni.usc.edu
  Learn about your brain (70 000 thoughts per day).
- University of Kent Careers and Employability Service
  http://www.kent.ac.uk/careers/ivdress.htm
  Interview style guide.
- Prospects
  http://www.prospects.ac.uk/interview_tips_assessment_centres.htm
  Interview tips.

What to do next

Ask a friend to practise the speed interrogation questions with you. Start training your mind through relaxation and visualisation. Research the dress code for your favourite employers.

Peak performance

Contents

The 'performance' word can be a problem. It seems that as a candidate you are constantly exhorted to be yourself. At the same time, you are assessed on your 'performance', which has a hint of something undignified and false.

You will notice the performance word is somewhat overused in assessment centre advice.

> 'Assessment centres assess your performance in a range of situations.'
> — *Prospects*[1]

> '… with any performance, practice makes perfect.'
> — *Guardian Jobs*[2]

'Performance' may suggest to you the idea of acting or putting on a show. However, it's better to consider the other meanings of 'performance'. It can just mean that someone is working well, performing his or her role. Change your interpretation of the 'performance' word. Performance in the assessment centre context is mainly:

- You being your best.
- You on a good day.

This will help you to be more comfortable with the idea of performing and allow you to focus on delivering a true-to-yourself, peak performance.

Performance awareness

Projection is performance

In simple terms, what you project outwards in your physiology, what shows on your face and body, is in fact your 'performance'. That's the impression you're giving. When nerves take over your mind, the impression or performance is polluted and actually misleading. You are allowing yourself to present yourself inaccurately. So, what you think inside your head consciously or subconsciously, is revealed as a negative vibe from your physiology and in your demeanour.

There is a useful mind-bending technique (a different kind of cognitive rehearsal)[3] that can help prime the inside of your head. Call it an inside/outside approach.

An inside/outside approach

This is a relaxation technique that requires you to think back to a 'good memory'. Some people say that they do not find these mind exercises easy. What you *will* find is that if you practise them a bit, they become quite natural and almost effortless.

Most people can daydream without any conscious effort. This is an invitation to daydream and is actually a kind of mini trance. You are doing it to yourself.

Read the instructions first and then try it out.

'Remember a time when . . .' relaxation

1. Sit or lie comfortably in a quiet place.

2. Check through your body mentally. Tense and relax from your toes through your limbs and torso, to your face (let your tongue be loose inside your mouth), to your head and scalp.

3. Notice your breathing. Just observe it mentally.

4. Now, in this quiet state, allow yourself to remember a time when you were happy or successful at something or just recall a really good day. Let your mind find something positive.

5. Let yourself *see what you saw* that day. You might get a picture. You might see yourself or others. Whatever comes to mind is fine.

6. Let yourself *hear what you heard* that day. There may be sounds or music or voices. You may hear your own voice.

7. Let yourself *feel what you felt* that day. Recapture the feeling.

8. Hold onto this memory gently and enjoy the recall of it.

9. Bring yourself gently back to the present.

10. Open your eyes.

A positive memory anchor

Now this all might seem a bit new age and self-indulgent, but what you have just recreated for yourself is a positive memory anchor. You can use this any time you want to recharge yourself for a challenge (an interview or assessment centre) or after a knock-back. It is de-stressing and beneficial for your mind to indulge in this type of activity. The *see/hear/feel* sequence is a sensory invitation that utilises different parts of your brain. It imprints a positive state in your psyche. It is actually the opposite of a phobia, which is a negative imprint state.

If you were to video yourself, or someone else, doing this 'Remember a time' exercise, you would notice how the person's external physiology changes. There would be a radiated sort of glow coming from the person. There would be a positive energy, signalled by the person's face and body language.

This uses a recalled cognitive state to change your current mindset. Practise this regularly and you will develop an ability to take control of your own mind.

Charge yourself up

You can then use this just before you go into an interview to focus your mind. By doing this any time you need to feel charged up, you will ensure that what is observable or perceived (from your physiology) by assessors or interviewers is a positive vibe.

To sum up:

Chapter 12

What you think on the inside shows on the outside.
So make sure you take control of your thinking.

An outside/inside approach

You've worked on the inside of your head, resetting your thoughts (the inside/outside approach). You can double up the effect of this resetting by taking an outside/inside approach.

If you've ever felt a bit down or just bothered by something or someone, you might have noticed that a bout of exercise can change this mental state. This change is triggered through the power of your endorphins. Exercise triggers endorphins, the chemical neurotransmitters in your brain that cause a euphoric feeling. If you want to put yourself in a revved-up state, activating those endorphins is a smart thing to do.

What's interesting is that you can work on the inside of your head through cognitive rehearsal and mindfulness techniques and also take this outside/inside approach. This would involve you doing something physically active to prepare for an interview or assessment centre. Take a look at these ideas.

An outside/inside approach

Go to the gym, shower and dress for your interview.

Go for a run, shower and dress for your interview.

Do some gentle yoga stretches, shower and dress for your interview.

Walk to the interview.

Do star jumps, wave your arms around, laugh or do something similar, and then go to the interview.

Do something else that you can think of that you know will energise you (you don't have to reveal this!).

This is not a recommendation for doing an iron man challenge or triathlon. Aim for exercise that invigorates without utterly exhausting you. The release of endorphins generated by gentle exercise may just give you the energy boost and happy mood that will come across powerfully in assessment centre or interview challenges.

Voice work

Most people realise that body language or physiology 'speaks' in its own way. However, your tonal delivery, the way you speak, is almost as important as what you say.

Recalling your 'good memory' state will also help your voice. The relaxation aspect will ease tension in your throat muscles, allowing your voice to project better and have greater smoothness and resonance. Think of your voice as a precious instrument.

There are ways to help your voice project in a clearer, more positive way. Try this next activity to make you more aware. You are going to test your voice out, speaking the same phrase, after different exercises. It is useful to record each spoken phrase on a device. Listen to this recording later. You will notice some differences.

Chapter 12

Self-awareness: What affects your voice projection?

1. Follow the instructions for each exercise.
2. Then speak the sentence below.

   The sentence: '**I know this is the perfect job for me.**'

   Exercise 1 – Sit slightly slumped in a chair. Speak the sentence.

   Exercise 2 – Pull yourself up in the chair, and press the base of your spine to the back of the chair. Speak the sentence.

   Exercise 3 – Drink a half glass of water. Speak the sentence.

   Exercise 4 – Do some rounds of calming breathing. Speak the sentence.

   Exercise 5 – Find some music that you love and sing along loudly. Speak the sentence.

3. Listen back to your recordings. Are they all the same, or are their subtle or even obvious differences?

What did you discover? Did you work out what made your voice project better? For most people, the following aspects improve their vocal projection:

Posture Aim to stand or sit tall. Stretch your spine. Keep your head balanced with your chin parallel to the floor. Rotate your shoulders lightly so the shoulder blades are dropped down. Place the base of your spine against the bottom of the chair back if seated.

Vocal chords They need to be moist, not dry, so a small amount of water is beneficial. They also need to be warmed up. Singing helps.

Lungs and chest Lungs need to be free to power the breath out, so avoid tight waistbands and slouching. The chest area needs to be relaxed. Breathing practice helps.

Finally, with regard to voice quality, you have to believe what you are saying about yourself. All the self-awareness exercises are aimed at developing your own understanding and belief of your own uniqueness.

Remember how you prepared for

- guessing the questions that you will be asked and
- framing your responses.

This will help you develop fluency in articulating your absolute suitability for the job role. In that way, your voice and your self-belief will complement each other. You will seem genuinely confident.

Confidence boosters

Graduate recruiters sometimes complain that candidates lack the skills they require.[4]

Think about this. What might be behind this statement? Perhaps graduates have not developed the right skills through their time at university. Perhaps universities are to blame. Perhaps students need to do more to develop these skills. However, it may just be that graduates are not demonstrating these skills confidently. Perhaps they possess these skills but are not confident about 'showing' them off to recruiters.

Confidence perceptions

A common reason given for failure at an interview or assessment centre by graduate applicants is lack of confidence.

> ### My story – Chris Jackson, experience of an accountancy assessment centre
>
> We were all asked to introduce ourselves to the group. That was awkward, and I didn't think I did this well.
>
> In the group exercise, everyone had ideas, and often I would come up with an idea and find someone else had just offered it.
>
> I did not get through to the afternoon interview, but I was not surprised at this. Others seemed to be so much more confident.

You might believe that some people are confident and some just aren't. The idea that confidence is something you have or do not have suggests it's a fixed capacity. That's one perception.

What if confidence was not a defined and limited quantity, but a behaviour you could choose? If it was an actual behaviour you could choose, you could be confident about choosing to act confidently.

What's noticeable is this:

- People who say they lack confidence are always confident about their lack of confidence.
- People who say they lack confidence often have bits of confidence in other parts of their lives, which they overlook.

It may all seem like semantic trickery, but psychologists understand that this ill-defined thing called confidence is

- something that some people can be born with (a bit of genetics) and
- something that can be developed.

Acting as if

Research into successful people throws up some interesting insights. It seems that people who appear confident often claim to feel like they are 'acting' confident and will be found out. However, this 'acting as if' type of confidence is often convincing, an effective 'trick' and a good way of priming your mind and behaviour (a further stage of cognitive rehearsal).

Chapter 12

It would seem that by 'acting as if' you are confident, you might find the way to develop confidence. Instead of just thinking yourself confident (positive thinking and cognitive rehearsal), you could practise 'acting as if' you are confident, often referred to as the positive action approach or the 'As If principle' (Wiseman 2012).[5]

So try some 'acting as if'. Before you go in to an assessment centre or interview, choose your own confident behaviour (how you would like to be), and activate your own positive action mode.

Dealing with setbacks

Most people are not ready for the sheer slog of the recruitment marathon or the constant knock-backs. However capable you are as an individual applicant, the likelihood is that you will make great applications and yet miss out often by a hair's breadth.

Each time you will have to re-energise yourself for the next trial while not allowing any diminishment of your own self-belief. This ability to bounce back is referred to as resilience and is the subject of many psychological studies.

Evidence suggests that to develop this quality you will need a particular attitude:

- A sense of *control* over your own destiny (you see yourself in the driving seat).
- A sense of *commitment* to your own goals (you are ready to persist in the face of obstacles).
- A *challenge* mindset (you see a setback as a challenge)[6].

(This framework can be found on the Centre for Confidence website *www.centreforconfidence.co.uk*, which is a good resource for research about confidence and resilience.)

These are attitudes you can choose to foster as you go through the application and assessment processes.

Take a look at the story of a very determined applicant.

It is fairly obvious that this candidate had the resilience and persistence required to gain a first role with this popular employer. Think about how you can use your mind to keep yourself motivated so that your performance in any stage of the recruitment process allows you to blow away the competition.

My story – Katherine Gumeniuk, Sports Producer, SKY

I studied media and television production at university, and during my time studying, I emailed so many television companies, begging for work experience. For the 100 you email, you may only get two replies!

The first time I emailed Sky Sports for work experience, I actually got turned down, but as a massive sports fan I really wanted the work experience with Sky. I continued to email Sky Sports, and finally I was given a week during my final year at university. I came down to London and remember feeling more excited than nervous.

The work experience was fantastic and really invaluable. I used my time very wisely during my work experience and managed to interview several female Sky Sports news presenters, whose interviews I later transcribed and used in my dissertation.

On my last day of work experience, one of the assistant producers I had worked with on *Soccer AM* asked me if I had enjoyed the week and if Sky was a place where I could see myself working in the future, and of course I answered *yes*! I was then called up to the production coordinator's desk (who was the person work experience placements reported to) and was offered a position as a runner once I had completed my degree! I remember feeling so overwhelmed but so happy.

It's also worth focusing on ways to boost your brainpower overall as you go through interviews and assessment activities. Your memory muscle will need to be in peak condition.

Memory boosters

Any kind of assessment centre or interview process is a memory challenge worthy of a memory champion, so borrow some of the established techniques they use.

Remembering a list

Use the method of loci. Think of a familiar place such as your house or route to work. Imagine each list item in a room of your house or at a point on the way. Make it memorable by putting the item in a funny or ridiculous setting.

Here's an example. Megan has a list of her five best aptitudes which she wants to remember. She has five rooms in her flat. She walks herself through it in her mind, placing each aptitude in a different room.

Memory Method 1: Loci		
Room	**Aptitude**	**Memory Tag**
Hall	Outgoing	She sees herself in her hall, singing operatically to the neighbours.
Kitchen	Efficient	She sees herself in her kitchen, next to a hill of chopped carrots.
Bathroom	Good communicator	She sees herself in the bath, talking earnestly to a rubber duck.
Lounge	Organised	She sees her books on the bookshelf, colour-coded by author.
Bedroom	Creative	She sees a giant artist's easel perched on the middle of her bed.

Now, she has to practise walking through the flat in her mind, allowing the memory tags to prompt her memory. Try this out for yourself. It is a highly effective technique for remembering a list and surprisingly fun to do.

Make your own mnemonics

You may have used these techniques to help your exam performance. A mnemonic is just a memory aid.

Try to create an acrostic. Take the first letter of something you want to remember and build a silly sentence out of it (rearrange the letters to make a sentence). For example you might want to remember to say that you have experience of:

- Computer coding
- Negotiating contracts and bids

- Numerical aptitude
- Project management
- Arguing/debating
- Presenting complex data.

Your silly sentence might be:

Canaries **N**ever, **N**ever **P**ee **A**t **P**ostmen

Similarly you could make up an acronym, which is one word where each letter is a reminder. For example – you might want to use the word 'explore' to remember five important things you like about a company for your interview. They might be:

Expertise

Place of work

Opportunities (career)

Reputation

Energy industry

Try these techniques out if you need to imprint a particular list or sentence in your mind.

Finally, it is worth trying a final awareness exercise to alert you to your own motivations for your career. This will help you apply for the right job roles. It will give you the ability to articulate your motivation for a particular career. It will help you perform authentically in any stage of the assessment process.

Career motivation

Start by imagining your future career as segments of a circle. Decide what your career will have to give you, in terms of opportunity to develop and be happy – your career motivators.

Here's an example. This is how one graduate completed a career motivation circle. The six segments represent what she wants ideally in her career.

Chapter 12

Example: Career motivation circle

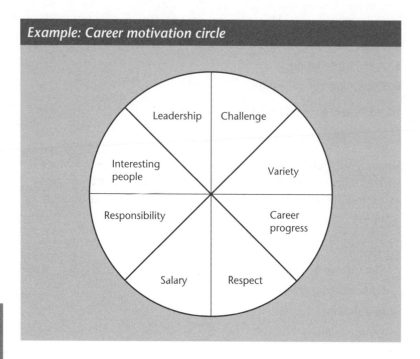

Now you try this exercise. Look at the list of common career motivators. Pick eight from the list, or come up with your own ideas.

Common career motivators		
Status	Excitement	Leadership
Security	Achievement	Interesting people
Challenge	Responsibility	Making a difference
Salary	Career progress	Helping others
Variety	Independence	Ethics
Curiosity	Teamwork	Wealth

Self-awareness: Career motivation circle

1. Think of eight important elements that would make up your ideal career.
2. Note them down in the boxes in each segment.

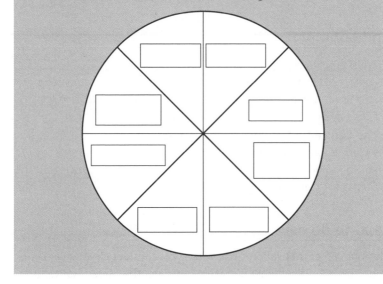

Keep these career motivators in mind when you apply for graduate roles and go through various recruitment processes. These represent your core career drivers. Revisit your career circle regularly to fix these in your mind. You might even change your mind at some point.

The self-knowledge that you gain from this exercise will prepare you for applications, assessment activities and interviews. It will help you deliver a peak performance.

Motivating yourself

If you mean to crack the recruitment nut, you will need to know what you want (Career Motivation Circle) and set your goals for your own version of a meaningful life. So many graduates get knocked off track

Chapter 12

due to setbacks and the natural, brief despondency that sets in when university is over. Be convinced that you will achieve your career goals if you exert yourself. Practise persistence and proactivity. You can create the career life you deserve. Go forth and be brilliant – nothing less is allowed!

Find out more

- **Train your memory**
  Foer, J. 2011. *Moonwalking with Einstein*. London: Penguin Press. To learn more about your memory and how to train it, read Josh Foer's book.
- **The Centre for Confidence and Well-Being**
  www.centreforconfidence.co.uk
  For tools and techniques to build confidence and resilience, visit the Centre for Confidence.

What to do next

Use your career motivation circle when you consider a particular career or job role. Check whether it is likely to deliver the career motivators you need.

References

Chapter 01

1. 'Future fit – Preparing graduates for the world of work'. 2009. CBI. www.cbi.org.uk/media/1121435/cbi_uuk_future_fit.pdf.
2. 'Do something good today'. Do-It.org https://do-it.org/.
3. UN Volunteers. onlinevolunteering.org. https://www. onlinevolunteering.org/en/index.html.
4. 'Headline statistics'. 2013–14. HESA (Higher Education Statistics Agency). https://www.hesa.ac.uk.
5. 'The Graduate Market in 2014'. High Fliers Research Ltd. 2014. www.highfliers.co.uk/download/GMReport14.pdf.
6. '85 applicants – or more – per graduate job'. 2013. AGR (Association of Graduate Recruiters), July 11. www.agr.org.uk/ corecode/search/search.aspx?term=85%20applicants.
7. 'The Graduate Market in 2013'. High Fliers Research Ltd. 2013. www.highfliers.co.uk/download/GMReport13.pdf.
8. FSB (Federation of Small Businesses) Statistics. www.fsb.org.uk/ stats.
9. The Sunday Times Best Companies. http://features. thesundaytimes.co.uk/public/best100companies.
10. Glassdoor: Get Hired. Love Your Job. www.glassdoor.co.uk.

Chapter 02

1. Self-Selection Tool – NHS Graduate Management Scheme http:// www.nhsgraduates.co.uk/application/hints-and-tips.aspx.
2. 'The Graduate Market in 2014'. High Fliers Research Ltd. 2014. http://www.highfliers.co.uk/download/GMReport14.pdf.
3. Association of Graduate Recruiters (AGR) Winter Survey 2014. http://www.agr.org.uk/write/Documents/Surveys/The_AGR_ Graduate_Recruitment_Survey_2013_Winter_Review.pdf.

4. 'Thirty-seven percent of companies use social networks to research potential job candidates, according to new CareerBuilder Survey'. 2012. CareerBuilder, 18 April. http://www.careerbuilder.com/share/aboutus/pressreleasesdetail.aspx?id=pr691&sd=4%2F18%2F2012&ed=4%2F18%2F2099.
5. Reppler research. 2011. https://www.reppler.com/learn/.
6. Google Alert. https://www.google.co.uk/alerts.
7. Reppler Social Media Monitoring. www.reppler.com.
8. Reppler research. 2011. https://www.reppler.com/learn/.
9. Duckworth, AL, Peterson, C, Matthews, MD and Kelly, DR. 2007. 'Grit: Perseverance and passion for long-term goals', *Journal of Personality and Social Psychology*, 92(6), 1087–1101.
10. Grit Test (Duckworth). https://sasupenn.qualtrics.com/jfe/form/SV_06f6QSOS2pZW9qR.

Chapter 03

1. Chamberlain, L. 2015. 'Assessment centres remain popular recruitment tool despite cost'. *Personnel Today*, 15 September. http://www.personneltoday.com/hr/assessment-centres-remain-popular-recruitment-tool-despite-cost/.
2. 'The Graduate Market in 2014'. High Fliers Research Ltd. 2014. http://www.highfliers.co.uk/download/GMReview14.pdf.
3. Seligman, M. 2006. *Learned Optimism: How to Change Your Mind and Your Life*. New York: Vintage Books.
4. Dijksterhuis, A and Knippenberg, A. 1998. The relation between perception and behaviour. *Journal of Personality and Psychology*, 74(4), 865–877.
5. The AGR Graduate Recruitment Survey. 2013. www.agr.org.uk.
6. 'Passing the skills tests'. Get Into Teaching, Department for Education. http://www.education.gov.uk/get-into-teaching/apply-for-teacher-training/skills-tests.
7. Digman, JM. 1990. Personality structure: Emergence of the five-factor model, *Annual Review of Psychology*, 41, 417–440.
8. 'Guidelines and information'. 2014. The British Psychological Society. http://ptc.bps.org.uk/ptc/guidelines-and-information.

Chapter 04

1. Dweck, C. 2012. *Mindset: How you can fulfil your potential.* London: Constable & Robinson.
2. Csikszentmihalyi, M, Rathunde, K, and Whalen, S. 1997. *Talented Teenagers: The Roots of Success and Failure.* Cambridge: University Press.
3. BBC Skillswise: English & maths for adults. 2015. http://www.bbc.co.uk/skillswise/maths.

Chapter 05

1. BBC Skillswise: English & maths for adults. 2015. http://www.bbc.co.uk/skillswise/topic-group/sentence-grammar.
2. WSJ, How Fast Can You Read This? http://projects.wsj.com/speedread/.
3. A.Word.A.Day. Wordsmith.org: The magic of words. https://www.wordsmith.org/awad/.

Chapter 06

1. 'The Graduate Market in 2014'. High Fliers Research Ltd. 2014. http://www.highfliers.co.uk/download/GMReview14.pdf.

Chapter 07

1. 'The Graduate Market in 2014'. High Fliers Research Ltd. 2014. http://www.highfliers.co.uk/download/GMReview14.pdf.
2. 'Future Fit – Preparing graduates for the world of work'. 2009. CBI. www.cbi.org.uk/media/1121435/cbi_uuk_future_fit.pdf.
3. 'Surviving the Assessment Centre'. 2012. jobs.ac.uk. February. http://www.jobs.ac.uk/careers-advice/interview-tips/1821/surviving-the-assessment-centre.
4. 'Client Care Information'. The Law Society, 26 March. www.lawsociety.org.uk/advice/practice-notes/client-care-letters.
5. Companies House. https://www.gov.uk/government/organisations/companies-house.
6. ThinkBuzan. http://thinkbuzan.com/.
7. 'AGR Global mindset, 2014. http://www.agcas.org.uk/agcas_resources/401-Global-Graduates-into-Global-Leaders

Chapter 08

1. 'The Graduate Market in 2014'. High Fliers Research Ltd. 2014. http://www.highfliers.co.uk/download/GMReview14.pdf.
2. Duncker, K. 1945. 'On problem-solving'. Lees, Lynne S. (Trans). *Psychological Monographs*, 58(5), i–113. http://dx.doi.org/10.1037/h0093599.
3. De Bono, E. 1990. *The Mechanism of Mind*. New York: International Centre for Creative Thinking.

Chapter 09

1. Croston, G. 2012. 'The thing we fear more than death'. *Psychology Today*, 29 November. http://www.psychologytoday.com/blog/the-real-story-risk/201211/the-thing-we-fear-more-death.
2. Altiero, J. 2006. *No More Stinking Thinking*. London: Jessica Kingsley Publishers.
3. Prezi. https://prezi.com/explore/staff-picks/.
4. Bounds, A. 2010. *The Jelly Effect: How to Make Your Communication Stick*. Chichester: Capstone Publishing.
5. LeVan, AJ. 2009. 'Seeing is believing: The power of visualization'. *Psychology Today*, 3 December. http://www.psychologytoday.com/blog/flourish/200912/seeing-is-believing-the-power-visualization.
6. '7–11 breathing: How does deep breathing make you feel more relaxed?' 2012. Human Givens blog, 26 October. http://blog.humangivens.com/2012/10/how-does-deep-breathing-make-you-feel.html.

Chapter 10

1. Skype. www.skype.com.
2. Seligman, MEP. 2003. *Authentic Happiness: Using the New Positive Psychology to Realise Your Potential for Lasting Fulfilment*. New York: Simon and Schuster.
3. Brenner, M. 2013. 'What is thought leadership? 5 steps to getting it right'. Forbes, 30 January. http://www.forbes.com/sites/sap/2013/01/30/what-is-thought-leadership-5-steps-to-get-it-right/.

4. Driscoll, J. 2000. *Practising Clinical Supervision: A Reflective Approach*. London: Balliere Tindall.
5. 'What to expect'. 2015. Nuclear Graduates. http://www. nucleargraduates.com/training/what-to-expect.
6. Goffman, E. 1990. *The Presentation of Self in Everyday Life*. London: Penguin.
7. Leary, MR. 1996. *Self-presentation: Impression Management and Interpersonal Behaviour*. Boulder, CO: Westview Press.
8. Jarrett, C. 2014. 'The psychology of first impressions'. *BPS Research Digest*, 22 July. http://digest.bps.org.uk/2014/07/the-psychology-of-first-impressions.html.

Chapter 11

1. Goffman, E. 1990. *The Presentation of Self in Everyday Life*. London: Penguin.
2. Winerman, L. 2005. '"Thin slices" of life'. *American Psychological Association*, 6(3), 54. http://www.apa.org/monitor/mar05/slices. aspx.
3. Ambady, N and Rosenthal, R. 1992. 'Thin slices of expressive behaviour as predictors of interpersonal consequences: A meta-analysis'. *Psychological Bulletin*, 111(2), 256–274. http://web. stanford.edu/group/ipc/pubs/1992Ambady.pdf.
4. Bernieri, FJ and Petty, KN. 2011. 'The influence of handshakes on first impression accuracy'. *Social Influence*, 6(2), 78–87.
5. Jarrett, C. 2014. 'The psychology of first impressions'. *BPS Research Digest*, 22 July. http://digest.bps.org.uk/2014/07/the-psychology-of-first-impressions.html.
6. Rowh, M. 2012. 'First impressions count'. *American Psychological Association*, November. http://www.apa.org/gradpsych/2012/11/ first-impressions.aspx.
7. McAleer, P. 2014. 'New research reveals the secret to making a good first impression'. *University News*, 13 March. http://www. gla.ac.uk/news/headline_312691_en.html.
8. McAleer P, Todorov, A and Belin, P. 2014. 'How do you say "hello"? Personality impressions from brief novel voices'. *PLoS ONE*, 9(3). http://journals.plos.org/plosone/article?id=10.1371/ journal.pone.0090779.

9. Collett, P. 2004. *The Book of Tells*. London: Bantam Books.
10. Laboratory of Neuro Imaging. www.loni.usc.edu.
11. Jarrett, C. 2014. 'The psychology of first impressions'. *BPS Research Digest*, 22 July. http://digest.bps.org.uk/2014/07/the-psychologyof-first-impressions.html.
12. Kirton, H. 2015. 'High proportion of graduate employers still can't fill vacancies, finds AGR'. CIPD Blog, 27 January. http://www.cipd. co.uk/pm/peoplemanagement/b/weblog/archive/2015/01/27/ high-proportion-of-graduate-employers-still-can-t-fill-vacancies-finds-agr.aspx.

Chapter 12

1. 'Interview tips: Assessment centres'. 2015. Prospects, June. http:// www.prospects.ac.uk/interview_tips_assessment_centres.htm.
2. 'Job interview tips: Expert advice for graduates.' 2011. theguardianjobs, 2 August. http://jobs.theguardian.com/ article/4340022/job-interview-tips-expert-advice-for-graduates/.
3. LeVan, AJ. 2009. 'Seeing is believing: The power of visualization.' *Psychology Today*, 3 December. http://www.psychologytoday.com/ blog/flourish/200912/seeing-is-believing-the-power-visualization.
4. 'Our latest research findings: The cognitive conundrum for graduate recruiters'. 2015. CEB: SHL Talent Measurement. http:// ceb.shl.com/Graduate-Intelligence/resources/; Paton, Graeme. 'University leavers lack the essential skills for work, employers warn'. *The Telegraph*, 12 September 2013. http://www.telegraph. co.uk/education/educationnews/10306211/University-leavers-lack-the-essential-skills-for-work-employers-warn.html.
5. Wiseman, R. 2012. *The As If Principle*. New York: Free Press.
6. Centre for Confidence and Well-Being. www.centreforconfidence. co.uk.

Index